Readings
on Groupwork Intervention
in Child Sexual Abuse

edited by

Andrew Kerslake

Whiting and Birch Ltd

MCMXCV

Published by Whiting & Birch Ltd,
PO Box 872, , London SE23 3HL, England.
USA: Paul & Co, Publishers' Consortium Inc,
PO Box 442, Concord, MA 01742.
British Library Cataloguing in Publication Data.
A CIP catalogue record is available from
the British Library
ISBN 1 871177 51 0 (cased)
ISBN 1 871177 40 5 (limp)
Printed in England by Antony Rowe, Chippenham

60 0412274 X

Readings on Groupwork Intervention
in Child Sexual Abuse

Swindon

Contents

An introduction to groupwork intervention in child sexual abuse

Andrew Kerslake

The articles in this collection of readings on child sexual abuse and groupwork have been drawn from recent editions of two British journals, 'Groupwork' and 'Practice', plus one original paper. They are not intended to represent an overview of this approach to intervention, indeed a number of areas of known work are significant by their absence. The aim is simply to bring together a range of work which can illustrate the potential of a groupwork approach and stimulate discussion on how best to build models of practice.

The necessity for this type of collection can be seen from the recent Department of Health publication *Working with Child Sexual Abuse: Guidelines for Trainers and Managers in Social Services Departments*. In what is clearly a valuable and significant document for those working in British state sector social work there are a number of chapters which list and describe the training agenda for a range of staff.

1

Of primary relevance to practitioners is likely to be the chapter entitled *Training in Continuing Work and Treatment*. An interesting characteristic of this section is its constant use of the word 'treatment', as if there is a common acceptance and understanding of this term in work with, either those abused, or abusers. There is only a fleeting reference in the last two paragraphs to two or three different methodological approaches. Whilst not wishing to deny the importance of the document, this limited approach to describing and discussing treatment would appear to be increasingly symptomatic of the British approach to intervention.

It was noticeable that as child sexual abuse increasingly came to attention in the 1980s, fuelled by some well documented public enquiries, so the emphasis of state involvement has come to mean investigation, detection and assessment. Therefore, we now have a panoply of legislation, rules, regulations and procedures designed to cover all of the above. It is almost as if in our uncertainty about the efficacy or effectiveness of treatment, or even maybe our inability to decide between approaches, that detection and documentation has become a substitute for being able to 'treat', 'cure' or 'change' its victims or perpetrators. The argument is that both types of practice are essential, if we are not simply to end up detecting the existence of sexual abuse rather than ameliorating its effects or diminishing the likelihood of its (re)occurrence.

Given the overall dominance of individual or family contact between social workers and their clients it is noticeable that child sexual abuse is one area where groupwork appears to be assuming an increasing importance.

Kathleen Fuller, in her book *Child Sexual Abuse*, in talking about the United States says:

> In many respects group therapy is the intervention of
> choice in sexual abuse, and a variety of types of groups
> are being employed by practitioners providing service
> to sexually abused families.

Two of the papers in this publication put forward some of the reasons why groupwork is particularly appropriate. Craig in her project with female child 'victims' uses the work of Hindman to illustrate the appropriateness of groupwork. She sees it as being able to help:

- The victim to see that she is not responsible and that she has been manipulated into cooperation with the abuse.
- Releasing the victim from the power of the offender.
- Relieving guilt issues.
- Building self-esteem.

Similar benefits are also true as Erooga, Clark and Bentley argue in their work with perpetrators:

> Groupwork provides the opportunity for co-working,
> thus diminishing the risk (of the worker becoming
> enmeshed in the perpetrators view of the world and his
> abuse)... In addition, it enables each worker to sound
> out issues with colleagues and avoid collusion with the
> distorted thinking that every perpetrator presents. It
> also enables group members' uniqueness to be
> challenged by other group members thereby reducing
> the workers' helplessness in tackling denial and
> minimisation.

By reading the papers together a number of basic principles or groundrules begin to emerge regardless of the methodology being used.

These principles are common to many areas of groupwork:

Selection: Not only having a clear policy, but is groupwork at this time, for this person, the right response?

Staff: A need to be clearly committed to a groupwork approach. Groupwork during the day to emphasise its work component.

Access: Particularly for victims, offering transport to provide security and demonstrate the importance of the group.

Purposes: Making the purposes and goals of the group clear and explicit, re-emphasising why people are there.

Methodology: Knowing what you are doing and why you are doing it. Being able to replicate methods from one group to the next. Within the group focusing feelings where they belong.

Confidentiality: Setting clear boundaries to the group. With perpetrators, clearly establishing the meaning of trust.

Use of outside consultants: The need for co-workers to have a clearly identified person outside the group.

None of the above is intended to suggest exclusivity, indeed some of the papers clearly express the need for groupwork to be used as one of a number of responses.

Overall the aim of this publication, like so many others, is that people learn ideas and approaches, that they can further develop, to widen their own ability to tackle problems. The fact that it is about groupwork and child sexual abuse is a secondary consideration. Without methodologies that are implementable, sustainable and replicable there is no social work practice, only procedural imperatives and paid helpfulness. Groupwork may only have a marginal effect on the amount or inevitability of child sexual abuse. Its causes, as many publications can demonstrate, are heavily embedded in the fabric of our society. What these papers can demonstrate is that by carefully structured and targeted intervention it can begin to have an impact on some individual victims and perpetrators.

Andrew Kerslake SSRADU

One

Starting the journey:

Enhancing the therapeutic elements of groupwork for adolescent female child sexual abuse victims

Eileen Craig

BACKGROUND AND CONTEXT

The author is a team member in a small team of five social workers in an authorised child protection agency. The team provides a 24 hour child protection line and investigation service, as well as providing a management service to other agencies in Rochdale. This service involves holding a register and convening, chairing and minuting child protection case conferences. Since 1986, the author has been involved in a programme of group treatment for child victims of sexual abuse. She has co-worked each of these groups with a female professional from another agency, although she alone has been involved in all the groups.

The groupwork programme derives from the team's aim to provide an integrated treatment service. The team take the view that all family members, including the perpetrator, have the right to an offer of treatment when sexual abuse has occurred. Henry Giarretto's treatment and training programme in California has informed our programme (Giarretto, 1989). The Giarretto philosophy stresses the need, not only for integration of services, but the integration and co-ordination of all agencies involved with families where sexual abuse has taken place. Provision of clear support in the form of professionally led groups and sponsorship in the initial crisis are essential to the approach. Individual therapy is also provided where appropriate.

AIMS OF THE GROUPS

Victims of child sexual abuse are often left with feelings of responsibility for what has happened to them, and in some cases, for the breakup of their family. They are often fearful of their abuser, even where physical force has not been used, and suffer a loss of self-esteem. As a result they may be depressed, may overdose and self-mutilate, and experience difficulties in establishing intimate relationships. Even where children are not currently symptomatic, they welcome time and space to make some sense of their abuse.

The group had two simple but important general aims. The first was to provide a safe forum where victims could explore and resolve the feelings of isolation, shame and stigmatisation which result from the abuse. The second was to help the participants to break what Jan Hindman refers to as the 'trauma bond' with the offender. Hindman identifies six treatment goals which underpin the above two aims (Hindman, 1989):

1. 'Identifying the victim and offender': that is, helping the victim to see that she is not responsible, and that she has been manipulated into co-operation with the abuse. The author's involvement in work with offenders (see Bentley *et al.*, 1990) provided insight about 'grooming' of victims, which can be effectively used in clarifying issues of blame and responsibility.

2. 'Releasing the victim from the power of the offender': that is, breaking the trauma bond with the offender. Sharing in the group and making comparisons about the methods used to coerce them into their abusive situations can help the girls gain perspective on their abusers.

3. 'Relieving guilt issues': that is, for children who have subsequently come into care and whose siblings have come into care. They need reminding that family break-up is the responsibility of the perpetrator.

4. 'Building self-esteem': through body image work, learning how to take positive feedback from other group members, learning how to listen to, and really hear, compliments about themselves.

5. 'To break the cycle of sexual abuse': David Finkelhor's (1987) work confirms our experience that untreated victims of sexual abuse are more likely to take on a perpetrator as a partner.

6. 'Starting the journey from victim to survivor': often the whole process of discussing the group with their social worker, coming for assessment and talking about what it is they (the girls) might get out of the group, can be

the beginning of an important different way of dealing with their abuse. Many of them are at different stages on this journey and it is helpful for them in the group to see what is achievable.

Although the above aims provide the framework for the group and are the stated aims of the group leaders, girls often bring their own clear aims and objectives, even quite early on in the group. The group can usually accommodate these. For example, girls who face the prospect of giving evidence against their perpetrators in criminal trials may come to the group specifically wanting help in preparation for that. The benefits to an anxious girl in such a situation, of being able to share with another who has already been through the same ordeal, are considerable. One 14 year old girl in the group gave evidence against her grandfather, at great personal cost to herself, and he was subsequently found not guilty because the corroborative evidence was weak. However, this girl was able to express feelings of empowerment, derived from her ability to bring her grandfather to the position of being openly charged in court. Despite the outcome, she was able to take some strength and encouragement from the professionals, particularly the Police, who had believed and supported her. She believed she had made a statement to her grandfather that he no longer held power over her, which was all the more powerful for having been a public one.

Beyond the broader aims and objectives of the group, there is usually an agreed plan for each individual girl, which may start to be worked out at the first meeting with the social worker, but will be firmed up during the contracting period and developed through the life of the group.

RECRUITMENT AND SELECTION

We made mistakes in the early life of the group by admitting girls who were still in a state of shock and with little or no stability in their lives. Our criteria are constantly developing, but stability is important. An example may demonstrate why. One 14 year old, who prior to the group had disclosed longstanding sexual abuse by her natural father and had not been believed by her mother, was in residential care. She was glue-sniffing, constantly running away, and became sexually active with boys of her own age, intending to get pregnant. When she was actually in the group, she was co-operative, helpful and able to articulate her feelings, but her absences and lack of commitment to the group significantly affected the growth of trust, and seriously restricted the potential for healing for that particular girl. Evaluation also proved impossible as this girl missed the last few sessions of the group in order to avoid ending it.

The current criteria for the group are as follows:

1. Girls between 14 and 18 years of age who have been sexually abused within or outside of their families.
2. They must have stated a wish to join the group.
3. Potential members need to be able to confirm openly their status as a sexual abuse victim.
4. All necessary steps must have been taken by the appropriate professionals and/or carers to ensure that the girl is protected and not at risk from any further abuse.
5. Presence of some stability in the girl's life. This does not exclude girls who are in crisis following disclosure where they are being cared for by a trusted and believing adult.

Some adolescent victims of child sexual abuse find the idea of sitting in a room full of other victims at worst a nightmare, and at best a gruelling ordeal. Many of the girls who have committed themselves to our group programme do so against their better judgement. Some may still be denying their abuse, and/or its effects upon them, and the introduction of the subject may induce an intolerably high level of anxiety which needs to be dealt with on an individual basis, before groupwork is a possibility. However, for most of the girls, coming to the group means that they have chosen to deal with their feelings about the abuse, rather than avoid or deny them. This in itself is a huge step. It is often terrifying, and requires great courage and strength.

CONTRACTING WITH KEY WORKERS/ OTHER INVOLVED PROFESSIONALS

Making clear agreements with key workers from the outset, and giving as full as possible an account of the groups's aims and objectives and how they are achieved, ensures that all the professionals have realistic expectations of each other's roles. It serves to avoid situations where there is confusion about responsibility for carrying out various tasks.

Initial contracting with social workers, where one is involved, needs to be done at or immediately following the assessment interview and needs to cover the following areas:

1. That the worker understands and supports the aims of the group and the group leaders.
2. That the worker is committed to supporting the new member in making the group a priority.
3. Clarifying responsibility for ensuring the safe arrival

and return home of group members. For example, some girls may be afraid to travel alone in taxis, particularly for long distances. Who actually does this is less important than actually being clear about where responsibility lies, and getting a commitment to it.

4. Clear agreements about the status of shared information. Girls need to be made aware that information they share with group leaders, which has implications for their safety and well-being, will be shared with their social worker.

5. Clear understanding that further disclosures of abuse made by a young person in the group will be investigated by her key worker and not the group leaders.

6. Recognition that in the early life of the group, girls will prefer to discuss problems they may be encountering with their known worker. They are encouraged to do this and give permission to their worker to share that information with the group leaders.

The negotiation of this contract between the worker and the group leaders helps to prepare the girl for how things are done in the group and can provide a good experience of professionals working co-operatively in her best interests. The continued use of contracts is detailed in the description of the group.

STRUCTURE AND PROGRAMME

One of the most important pieces of learning from previous groups concerns length, frequency and timing. Previous groups had met fortnightly for an 11 month period with meetings taking place during the evening. This structure reflected the needs of the workers at the time and the demands of their agencies. However, it became clear that leaving girls for two weeks to hang on to issues that had been opened up in particular sessions resulted in much time being spent 'retrieving' material in the next session. In addition, meeting in the evening often meant that the workers were running the group at the end of a busy day when they were tired, emotionally less available, and disinclined to de-brief immediately after the group. In order to avoid these problems, the most recent group has met weekly for five months, each session taking place during the day. These changes have also had other benefits. The girls realised that they were seen as important because work with them was not relegated to time when other work was not going on. The power of this message was enhanced by the negotiations with schools and employers which were necessary to enable their attendance to take place during the day. The actual process of this negotiation, the openness of it, and our willingness to undertake it, has provided some effective modelling and helped to reduce the feeling of stigma that the girls experienced.

The first four sessions, referred to as the 'orientation phase', are tightly structured and, in the early stages of the group, we tend to plan in some detail. This provides a sense of safety and containment which reduces anxiety. As the group becomes more cohesive, we plan less, and work more with the material that is in the room.

Dealing with 'unfinished business' as creatively as possible can mean talking to empty chairs, writing letters which are never posted, or re-creating a situation through drama and giving it a different ending.

Many of the exercises and techniques we use are contained in a very practical work book by Sheila Ernst and Lucy Goodison (1981).

CO-LEADERSHIP, GENDER AND CONSULTATION

Because of the experiences of this client group, and the intensity of the resultant feelings, many of the dynamics of the abusive family will be played out within the group. Projections onto group leaders are common, and regardless of skills, consultation to these processes is essential if the group leaders are to ensure that:

1. Rejecting and persecutory behaviour is not played out.
2. Workers are not left with strong perpetrator projections or bad mother projections.
3. Workers are able to reflect back to individual members in the group, dysfunctional ways that they ask, or do not ask, for what they want.

Also dynamics in the group will be mirrored in the dynamics of the consultation session. Following several very flat sessions in the group with girls denying the existence of problems, the group leaders hesitantly related to their consultant how they had been laughing hysterically at the girls when they were de-briefing, being rude about some of them, and calling them names. The group leaders felt very ashamed of this behaviour and almost did not report it to their consultant. The consultant was able to reflect back that the flatness in the group may be connected with the girls not feeling able to show their bad sides to us, and that the workers needed to validate their own feelings of irritation, crossness and anger with the girls, if the girls were to be free to do this themselves in the group.

If the group leaders are not to be 'dustbins' for the feelings of group members, structures need to be in place for the group leaders to deal with the effects. De-briefing immediately after the group may take the form of tears, expressions of anger, or a good outburst of hysterical laughter. Mutual feedback on group leader performances in the group, given in a constructive way, helps build on skills and expertise.

Female co-leaders have been a feature of all of the girls' treatment groups on the basis that at this early stage in their treatment, presence of a male worker can be an inhibiting factor. Many of the girls are learning to describe their abusive experiences for the first time, and some have expressed fears that the presence of a male worker would compound their feelings of shame and embarrassment. Our view is that some of the girls who have gone through two groups, and who are at a different stage in their treatment, could benefit from a male co-leader being in the group and providing them with a very different experience of a male adult.

BRIEF DESCRIPTION AND ANALYSIS OF ONE GROUP

The following is a brief review of one group which ran between March and November 1989. Nine girls were selected from assessment interviews where the criteria already described were applied. The abuse ranged from one girl who had been sexualised at the age of three years by her father leading to full intercourse at nine years and continued intercourse until disclosure at 14, to a 15 year old girl who was raped by her uncle, but as far as we knew, had not been previously sexually abused. All had been abused within their families. More than half had received violence or violent threats against them as a means of coercion. Three of the girls were living at home with their mothers, and the other six were in care.

These nine girls included two girls who had been members of a previous group. They were interviewed and assessed in the same way as the other potential members, and were clear that this was not a continuation of their previous group.

The group began with a four week orientation phase, meeting weekly. This orientation phase was concerned with testing out each individual's commitment to the group, establishing individual contracts, identifying the general rules of the group and enabling the girls to get to know each other and the leaders. At this stage one girl decided that she could not make a commitment to the group, and left. It is important to allow a choice at this stage in order to ensure that girls do not embark on something in which they are not willing participants and also to ensure that the group is stable for the rest of its life. The individual contract between each girl and the group leaders identified the main issues in their lives that they wished to work on and be helped with in the group. Certain themes are likely to be identified at this stage, particularly ambivalent feelings towards perpetrators and mothers, and feelings of shame, guilt, 'dirtiness' and worthlessness. Five of the remaining eight girls negotiated contracts around these areas. Two others contracted to work on preparation for giving evidence in court against their abusers.

The remaining girl who had been abused by several adults, including her mother, had great difficulty communicating with the group. Her contract was solely to be present at the group. In spite of going through several crises in her life, during the period of the group, she continued to attend.

This group did not contain any girls who had self-mutilated or attempted suicide, but previous groups had. We believe it is necessary in these circumstances to include a no harm/no suicide clause in the contract and to have this restated at each session. The group then offers a functional way for the girls to deal with the feelings that lay behind their self-mutilation/suicide attempt.

Contracting may also include areas of work not directly related to the sexual abuse. For example, one 17 year old girl who was joining her second group, and who had a very low self image, rarely washed her hair and wore dirty, boyish clothes. She agreed when contracting into the group, to pay more attention to herself and give herself treats like baths, hair washes, and new clothes when she could.

Body image work often entered into contracts in the form of feeling dirty and 'used'. Two girls in this group had quite specific feelings about their breasts and other parts of their anatomy, and were only able to identify these issues well into the life of the group, and work on these issues was then included in their contracts.

The leaders also contracted as part of this process. They agreed to be present each week, to be on time, to offer feedback during the sessions, to provide structure and to maintain confidentiality. Again, the group leaders agreed not to discuss the contents of the group with anyone other than the consultant, except where the safety or well-being of a girl was involved. We realised that this may have inhibited some group members from disclosing important information, but in our experience it is far more important not to risk a situation where a child feels that trust has been further betrayed.

This was mirrored in one of the general rules of the group, whereby the girls gave a clear agreement to each other that material they heard in the group was not for discussion with any person outside of the group. This was one of the three non-negotiable rules. The second was that the girls must not harm themselves or each other during the group. The third was a 'no-smoking, except during breaks' rule. This rule is not simply to do with health reasons, but to avoid situations where girls 'smoke their feelings away'. The group also established a rule that if a member missed two consecutive sessions, their continued membership of the group would be reviewed.

The remaining group 'joining' work comprised both a social element and exercises. From the outset, we believed it was important for the girls to feel valued and we started this process by ensuring that we were there to welcome the girls when they arrived. Food and drink were available for the first 15 minutes, and as the group progressed, this became a valuable part of the social element. Initially, some girls were too anxious to eat and drink together, and we were able to identify real progress in the relationship between group members when all the food and drink was consumed before the end of the 15 minutes!

We also found that this period was used by girls to make bids for the individual attention of the leaders through disclosure of information. This was occasionally dramatic and important information. One girl asked to see the group leaders in private, and then disclosed for the first time an additional episode of sexual abuse by an adult caretaker. She was encouraged to share this with the group who were then able to consider the process by which she had sought her individual attention from the group leaders. Motivation behind these kinds of incidents was not always immediately apparent and was more likely to be picked up in the consultation process. We used these bids to begin the process of looking at issues of the dysfunctional ways in which attention can be sought - ways which the girls used in other relationships.

At stated previously, the orientation phase is tightly structured, and the exercises we used as part of this structure were designed to break down barriers between group members and to provide opportunities for each girl to make some kind of contact with every other group member. Exercises done in pairs are particularly useful in this process. Some exercises involved physical touch, and for these we obtained permission from each girl. We agreed that all touch within the group must be open and talked about. This provided a contrast with their abusive experiences which would usually have been of covert, silent touching.

We had an opening and closing ritual for each session, established in the orientation phase. These were designed to help the girls ask for what they want in a straightforward way. The opening ritual was a simple exercise of 'how we are', where each girl would say something about how she was feeling at the particular moment, and might share something she had felt or experienced since the last group. If a girl had 'worked' or shared something important in the previous group, group leaders or group members might check out how she had been since. The concluding ritual was again a simple exercise (which I observed being effectively used in all of the Giarretto groups for both adults and children) where each girl gave some feedback to one other girl about how she had been in the group, and phrased the feedback in a way that allowed them to own it. Each girl was encouraged to make eye contact with the recipient of the feedback.

The latter exercise produced quite dramatic responses, although it was often initially resisted quite strongly. There was also a tendency for generalisations to be made rather than specific feedback, and time was needed to encourage each girl to complete the task. For example, one girl who often giggled and laughed when she was feeling sad and upset, shared her upset feelings with the group and cried about her mum. One of the other girls was able to say to her in the feedback at the end 'I liked the way you showed us your sad feelings'. In subsequent groups she was able to continue to shed tears of sadness about her mother's rejection. With the help of the other girls, a theme developed which enabled her to 'tell' her mother, in the group, how it had felt for her to be unloved and unwanted.

Post-orientation, as the group had become more cohesive, was less structured and the co-leaders worked with what was in the room and what the girls brought. If a girl asked for some time at the beginning of the group, or the group leaders picked up an issue from the round of how the girls were, then the group planned how it might best be dealt with. Discussion was an invaluable part of the group process, and a place where the girls learned to name their feelings, learn words for some of their experiences, and shared fears that they carried from early childhood. For example, one girl shared her deeply felt anxiety that she would never be able to physically have a baby because of her abusive experiences as a very small child. A full medical examination was arranged at her request, and after being reassured of no physical damage, she was able to explore more fully in the group the emotional component of her anxiety.

During this period, guided fantasies were used on two occasions to focus on locating parts of the body where certain feelings were lodged or stuck. Another useful exercise for this was for group members to draw life-size images of their bodies, using a partner to produce the outline. There needs to be trust established before this exercise is attempted, and some of the girls in this group found it impossible to lie on their back and allow someone to touch and draw round certain parts of their body.

This lack of trust can also be an issue during guided fantasy or relaxation work and can bring up important material to be worked on in the group. One girl who became quite rigid when encouraged to try to lie on her back and relax, was only able to lie and listen to the music in a foetal position.

Cushion work provided opportunities for 'safe' dialogue with perpetrators. Several girls reported a reduction in panic attacks, nightmares and general fearfulness after confronting their perpetrator in the form of a cushion. This always took great courage and often high levels of fear prevented the girl from actually saying any of the words to the cushion, although in the group setting she might be able to describe exactly what she would say, to the other girls. Although an excellent method of facilitating expressions of rage, it has been our experience that girls have needed to work through several layers of feelings, of sadness and despair, before they can undertake such work. If one of the girls was 'working' in this way, then one group leader would direct this and concentrate her attention on the girl. The other group leader would scan the group where, undoubtedly, issues would be resonating, and each girl was given the opportunity to share what was happening for her during the exercise.

Drama was another tool used once the group had become cohesive. The girls acted out court scenes where a potential witness played herself and selected her own legal advocate from amongst group members. A group leader played the abuser's lawyer and made provocative statements about the witness which reflected that girl's unspoken view of herself, *e.g.* 'You never told him to stop'. This enabled the 'witness' to acknowledge and explore her own worst fears about herself and get accurate and realistic feedback from the other girls.

EVALUATION

Evaluation takes several forms and in this particular group we asked professionals referring girls to tick boxes in an assessment form covering areas like, ability to express feelings (both generally and to do with the abuse), whether the girl avoided issues regarding her abuse, and attitude about self, both sexually and emotionally. Self abusive and other significant behaviours would also be noted here. An example would be 'how far is the child able to recognise how the abusive situation was maintained (for example, fear of father/mother, withdrawal of affection or privileges, protection of siblings or mother *etc.*?)'. Workers are given choices for an answer and asked to tick boxes - 'A lot', 'Moderate', 'A little', 'Needs work'. This assessment form is completed again at the end of the group and questions referring to group progress are also answered at this stage. Therefore, questions like, 'How far is the girl able to reach out to others for support (peers and group leaders)?', would now be answered. Where social workers or other professionals are not involved, the group leaders would complete the assessment forms.

Several of the girls improved their 'score' re ability to focus anger towards the appropriate person. Also there were noted changes for all the girls re their ability to express feelings about mothers. Each member made measurable progress in learning to not take responsibility for the above.

This professional assessment is used in the concluding interview with each girl's worker, to make recommendations for future treatment work.

The last three sessions of this group were used for self and peer evaluation. We used several simple exercises, some done in pairs and others done with the whole group, to facilitate the girls looking at specific changes that they felt they had made or others felt that they had made. Once more it was important to encourage the girls to be specific when they talked about being 'more confident' or 'less scared'. Often the difficult task of describing in detail how they might be different in one area promotes a deeper understanding of the changes made. As in other groups there were recurring messages about the good things to be had from the group. 'I'm not the only one', 'A knowing of trust', 'Learning to trust', 'Having someone to listen to me', 'A good feeling that I've helped someone else'. One girl reported that the most important change she had made was 'in learning not to bottle things up'.

Of the two girls who had contracted to do work on preparation for criminal court, only one gave evidence, as the Crown Prosecution Service decided not to proceed in the other case. Both girls said they had felt supported and strengthened by other group members, claiming that without it their respective experiences would have been intolerable. The group leaders' observations were that the girl who gave evidence made dramatic changes in the four months she spent preparing for court. Initially she had been unable to talk about the detail of her abuse without shaking, stammering or becoming totally withdrawn. By exploring and confronting the feelings which induced this state in the group, she was eventually able to give her evidence coherently and with minimal distress. In our view, with good support and preparation, the experience of giving evidence in court against an abuser can often be a therapeutic one.

Towards the end of this group, two girls began to write their stories in forms which they hoped one day might be published. Even if they are not, the group leaders felt justified in interpreting this as an indicator of success of the treatment.

We have consistently felt that there are observable and tangible positive short term effects for the girls who have been through our treatment programme. However, much follow-up (10-15 years) is needed to evaluate long term benefits.

CONCLUSION

There are obvious advantages in using group treatment for girls at this developmental stage, when peer influences are at their greatest. Also for child sexual abuse victims 'going public' in the group can be a safe rehearsal for giving up secrecy and shame in their lives outside. We believe that the safety provided by a well structured, clearly focused group can facilitate growth and change which can have a powerful and lasting impact on all of its members.

This article first appeared in *Groupwork*, 1990, 3(2)

Two

Groupwork with sexually abused boys

Alex Leith and Steve Handforth

INTRODUCTION

During the early part of 1987 the staff at the NSPCC Manchester Special Unit, through their involvement in chairing the child abuse case conferences, review meetings and consultations with colleagues, noted an increasing number of sexually abused boys being identified. It was noticeable that the workers engaged in individual work with the boys were finding it hard to achieve an effective therapeutic relationship. Therefore it was considered that a positive way forward might be the provision of a group where they could perhaps demonstrate acceptance and warmth for each other so assisting their move out of the role of 'victim' (Blanchard 1986).

Following the decision to offer such a resource, we outlined in a document circulated to a number of child care agencies our thoughts of how such a group might be structured and the issues we anticipated we would encounter. These were:

1. low self-esteem;
2. a reluctance to talk about the experience of abuse;
3. confusion about sexual identity;
4. feelings of self blame and guilt;
5. more general confusion about identity;
6. aggressive tendencies, springing from;
7. identification with the abuser.

We had identified these from the available literature (Freeman-Longo, 1986; Maltz and Holman, 1987; Pierce and Pierce, 1985; Reinhard, 1987; Rogers, 1984; Sebold, 1987) and our own experience of working with sexually abused children.

A number of referrals were subsequently received, from which a group of participants aged from 8 to 11 years was selected.

A particularly interesting point was that our circulated document, as we perceived it, generated a degree of suspicion and mistrust. This seemed to us connected to doubts about our motivation, the implication being that our interest in these boys was in some ways inappropriate. It may be helpful should other male workers engage in this work to acknowledge beforehand that this feature may be present and will have to be openly and honestly dealt with. We also experienced a sceptical response based on the thinking that as previous attempts to engage sexually abused boys in a group had failed, so would this attempt. Thus our experience has led us to believe that an essential prerequisite for recruiting boys to a group is clarity about the professional and personal motivation behind an involvement in this area of work.

This related to another issue considered at the outset, namely, the sex of the group leaders. Discussion took place in order to decide if two male workers would be appropriate. We acknowledge that there existed insufficient evidence in the literature and so we agreed to assess the position as the group developed. To that end we recruited a female consultant from the NSPCC/Greater Manchester County Child Sexual Abuse Unit, partly to allow introduction of a female group leader should that prove necessary. In this particular instance the two group leaders had previously worked together in a men's group and had developed trust in each other. This was deemed to be more important than the need to have a male and female leader.

It was made clear at the initial stages of discussion about the group that it would only be a part of the whole treatment package which was offered to a child. Key workers were asked to acknowledge that their role remained crucial. This was particularly so with regard to the key workers explaining to the families that attendance at the group might well resurrect feelings previously suppressed. It was the group leaders' expectation that the key worker would follow up with the family whatever difficulties they experienced between group sessions.

A total of six boys aged 8-11 years were eventually recruited for the group. All had been sexually abused and their experience included mutual masturbation, oral sex and full anal intercourse. The abuse often involved threats of violence and all the boys were reported to have been forced to participate in the abuse. A total of 13 weekly sessions were held each lasting a minimum of one and a half hours, some sessions lasting over two hours. The group leaders also transported the boys to and from the group with occasional help from colleagues. There was a strong commitment from the boys to the group and absences only occurred as a consequence of holidays or sickness. Attendance at the group was always good and never constituted a problem.

Initial stages

The value of consultation was highlighted after the first session when one of the features noted concerned the caution of the group leaders. This related to the absence of efforts to push the boys towards dealing with their specific experience of abuse. The group leaders had armed themselves with a repertoire of trust games and introductory exercises. These were not in fact needed and it became evident, even during the first session, that the boys were ready to tackle the issues involved arriving out of their abuse. While they might be hesitant and found it painful, they wanted to hear from each other what their experiences had been. The boys were fully aware of the purpose of the group and came to it expecting the leaders to help them focus on their abuse.

The initial stage of the group clearly focused the question of how the boys might need to be prepared for such a group. Our view is that once the abuse has been disclosed and investigated and a social worker is involved, that is likely to be sufficient preparation for attendance at a group.

When the group leaders first met the boys individually, all agreed to attend the group and said that they felt and knew that sharing with other boys who had been through the same sort of experience would be helpful. This was reinforced for them at the first session. Several themes quickly emerged, which then ran throughout the life of the group, and formed the focus of the work carried out.

ANGER

Unlike girls who have been sexually abused, where one issue is repressed anger (Sgroi, 1982), our experience in the boys' group was that the problems arose from constant and inappropriate expressions of anger. This was a feature common to all six boys and we noted that often people and agencies had avoided dealing with this through the use of holidays, outings and activity based exercises.

Both for us, as leaders, and the boys, as members of the group, this created a powerful sense of being ignored and in fact added to the level of anger present in the boys' lives. This in turn reinforced the aggressive behaviour within their peer group in school and in their families. The boys' anger arose directly out of their experience of sexual abuse, but it appeared that this had been suppressed during the course of the actual abuse. Once the abuse was disclosed the boys realised the extent to which the abuse was wrong. It was this aspect which resulted in them having an enormous quantity of anger that they felt they had to express.

One of the major problems was that the boys were unable to channel their anger where it belonged i.e. towards the abuser. In the group setting they often expressed anger towards each other, and occasionally towards the leaders, through obstructive behaviour. Continual efforts were made within the group to focus on the expression of anger towards the abuser. A number of techniques were used to assist this. The boys were encouraged to make plasticine models of the abuser, paint and draw the abuser, identify the abuser by name, throw soft objects at a blackboard upon which was drawn the abuser and write comments about the abuser on a graffiti board. It was interesting to note that much of the material on the graffiti board was sexual in nature. However equally important however, was the aggressive manner with which the boys carried out the task of writing their comments on the board.

The work done on anger involved the boys individually and collectively. As they became more secure within the group it became progressively easier for them to express their anger and channel it towards the abuser. This was, in our view, the first stage in our attempt to deal with the very real fear of the abuser. The presence of this fear caused the group leaders to become concerned that the boys might be entrenched in the role of victim. In an attempt to move them beyond this, no opportunity was provided for the expression of anger at one of the sessions. The consequence was an expression of anger outside the group and it was realised on reflection, through consultation, that such an opportunity needed to be provided at each session of the group.

The concern about the 'victim' role was also related to a specific concern about one particular boy who constantly placed himself in the role of victim within the group. Additionally, he then found it very difficult to extricate himself from this position, lacking the social skills necessary. Our view is that because of their experience of victimisation, it is likely that in any group of sexually abused boys, one will be selected somehow to play the role of victim. Efforts to protect the one placed in such a position need to be made and can provide a powerful demonstration of how the boys can help each other move beyond the experience of being a victim. As the group was forced to examine their behaviour towards the 'victim' they recognised a need in fact to protect and befriend him and so move him out of his 'victim' position. By helping him, the other boys were able to experience the good feelings attached to such behaviour and so were encouraged to allow other people to help them.

Thus after five sessions and after consultation the group leaders took the decision to move the group towards building up the boys' self-esteem and self-confidence. This was related to a growing realisation that the extent of the boys' anger, together with the limited time available, meant that the issues around anger were unlikely to be completely resolved. Linked to this was the awareness that it was appropriate to retain some anger. The main issue was how the anger could be expressed in the future. The group leaders felt that continuing feelings of hostility towards the abuser were to some extent appropriate, as long as the hostility remained focused on the abuser. Equally the boys' anger was seen as appropriate when it was linked to their efforts to develop a means of protecting themselves from any future abuse.

Thus although some anger remained at the end of the group, the group leaders' experience was that this could be used constructively, particularly in terms of combating the tendency of the boys to remain stuck in the role of victim. The remaining anger could also be channelled into efforts to ensure future protection.

IDENTITY

Our thoughts about a specific aspect of this, namely sexual identity, were influenced by the work carried out with a group of boys aged 15-18 years, who had been sexually abused. For them homosexuality and the whole question of sexual identity was a major issue.

Our experience of the younger boys' group was that the issue of sexual identity was not a major concern. We would concur with Blanchard's view that boys aged 12 years and under tend to focus on the issues of normal versus abnormal and those aged 12 years and over focus on issues of heterosexuality versus homosexuality. Therefore our experience in the two groups would lead us to believe that it is inappropriate to mix the two age groups.

As regards the younger boys, our experience was that they did describe some fears of being homosexual. However, we believe that if those fears can be dealt with at an early age then it is probable that the whole question of sexual identity does not become a major problem in later adolescence.

As regards the question of identity, one aspect that we noted in the younger boys' group was a feeling that the boys had in some way been damaged. A similar phenomenon has been reported by Suzanne Sgroi with reference to girls feeling that they were 'damaged goods'. Thus the boys described feelings of being 'like a piece of shit', a 'dick head', and of being 'broken in pieces'. Linked to this was what for the boys turned out to be a major question. That involved why they, as individuals, had been chosen to be victims. Carol Rogers (1984) describes boys as believing that their own physical appearance or personality caused the abuse. The result, which we ourselves experienced, is that the boys internalise the incident and so blame themselves for the abuse. They then feel in turn some way abnormal and feel that this can be physically recognised by other people outside.

Again our view was that by sharing in detail their particular experience of abuse and related fears, the group itself provided considerable reassurance to the boys that they were in fact normal. A great deal of checking out went on within the group and it was clearly evident when the boys realised that their own individual fears were not unique to them, they felt a powerful sense of reassurance.

A specific fear all the boys had was that their abuse may have resulted in them contracting Aids. All the boys had been tested and the knowledge that all the tests were negative, was a powerful source of reassurance. The boys reported that by sharing the experience of the fear of having Aids, of having to undergo the test and of having to await the results, any lingering doubts they might have had about whether they had been physically damaged was overcome by the experience of hearing the other boys go through the details, for example, of the relief at hearing the results of the tests.

Within the group a forum was provided for the boys to develop a more integrated sense of their own self worth. Exercises involving a jig-saw figure which represented themselves, constructive play, for example building a kite, and the use of a good/strong feeling graffiti board were all introduced to aid this. However, the most powerful source of enhanced self-esteem was a development of a strong group identity and the feeling of strong group cohesion. This allowed real personal sharing and it was this that the boys reported to be the most significant source of help.

Two further issues were specifically dealt with in relation to fears about identity. The first was their fear of being isolated, and the boys again reported that the experience of being a member of the group was a major source of comfort and enabled the boys to feel very much less isolated. The second related to their fear, and they described this as a real physical fear, of being abused again in the future. This was tackled through exercises designed to improve their ability to protect themselves. These exercises highlighted positive things that they could do as well as the things that they should not do.

Our experience of the group also highlighted another area of difficulty for the boys. This involved confusion arising out of the conflict between their advanced knowledge regarding sexual behaviour and of actual emotionally immature social behaviour. Whilst the boys were very 'street wise', their social skills were poorly developed. This created tension both for them and for other people around them. The group leaders attempted to aid resolution of this issue by offering a model of appropriate 'adult' behaviour and allowing the boys to behave in appropriately childish ways on occasions. However, this tension is in our view an important source of the boys' own personal difficulties and needs to be acknowledged by all adults who have contact with such children.

RELUCTANCE TO TALK

Prior to the boys attending the group, efforts had been made by individual workers to enable them to talk openly about their experiences. These efforts had not been particularly successful and the group leaders too, had initial difficulties in getting the boys to be explicit. This seemed to be directly related to their feelings of low self-esteem, guilt, shame, isolation and a general tendency to mistrust adults.

The group began by focusing on the feelings of isolation and it was the actual meeting with other boys who had been sexually abused, that allowed them to feel much less isolated. This then led very quickly to them sharing, which in turn enhanced group cohesion and this again encouraged further sharing. Initially the group leaders set up the graffiti boards and various exercises to encourage sharing. However, once the boys began to exchange details of their experiences and the reactions to the abuse and its disclosure, the need for such structure diminished. It was interesting to note that during the last session, at the boys' request, they once more described graphically their experiences of sexual abuse. The group leaders felt that the process of sharing in explicit detail the boys' experience, was in itself one of the most important sources of assistance for them. Via this process, they began to feel less guilty and shameful and felt more able to trust other people, whilst still being aware of the need to protect themselves from abuse in future.

IDENTIFICATION WITH THE ABUSER

By the fourth session of the group, this issue had already emerged. The group leaders had already been aware that two of the boys had sexually abused younger children. Then another boy began to express the view that he had in fact enjoyed the physical experience involved in the sexual abuse and believed that if he behaved in the same way towards another child, that child too would actually enjoy the physical experience. Thus it was clear that several group members were already moving, either in terms of thinking or in their actual behaviour, towards becoming sexual abusive themselves. A very early sign of the emerging pattern involved the comments which indicated a belief that they were unable to control their own behaviour. This seemed to be an honest interpretation involving no denial or rationalisation. This then gave the group leaders an opportunity to educate the boys about their behaviour, particularly through helping them to identify with their potential victims. By reference to their own experiences they were helped to contemplate the damage they could cause others if they abused someone younger than themselves. This also helped the two boys who had already abused other children begin to deal with their feelings of guilt. Our view is that by tackling this issue at a very early stage there was scope to challenge any identification that the boys were making with the abuser and the experience of being abused.

However, this proved to be more difficult for the boy who had begun to rationalise his thinking along the lines of providing physical pleasure for whoever he might abuse. Efforts were made to help him identify with the 'victim' experience. This proved to be quite difficult in terms of getting him to contemplate another child being a victim and suggests that once any rationalisation or denial of the experience of abuse occurs it becomes more difficult to prevent the process of identification with the abuser occurring.

For the group leaders this highlights the need for early identification and intervention when boys have been sexually abused.

ROLE OF THE NON-ABUSING PARENT

All the boys were resident with their natural mothers and all the men who had abused them were no longer resident in the family home. The abuse had, in all six cases, occurred within the family home. The men involved included fathers, co-habitees of the mothers, step-brothers and lodgers.

The boys reported that they did feel their mothers had some responsibility for failing to protect them from the abuser. They were considerably confused about their mothers' role as regards being to blame for the abuse. This seemed to mirror exactly the confusion felt by the mothers regarding their own feelings of guilt and blame for the abuse. This was evident on the occasions when the group leaders met the women and quickly picked up their anxiety about whether their sons were blaming them for the abuse. They sought reassurance from the group leaders that they were not to blame and clearly indicated their confusion. The key workers were then requested to continue to offer reassurance to the women. The group leaders' experience was that the mothers had very high expectations of the group, believing that the group might resolve all the family difficulties including their own personal ones.

Within the group, the process of channelling the boys' anger towards the abuser helped them understand better their mothers' position. While recalling how the abuser had behaved they were able to comprehend that it was possible for other people, including their mothers, to have been ignorant of the abuse. This together with the boys' increased self-esteem and diminished self-blame, aided a more realistic understanding of the mothers' position.

CONCLUSION

The original thinking behind setting up the group was that it would hopefully be a more effective way of helping the boys deal with the impact of their sexual abuse. The group leaders' experience confirmed the view that groupwork can be effective, but it needs to be allied to continuing individual work carried out with the boys, whether by the group leaders or other workers involved with the family. However, an additional benefit of the groupwork approach is that it clearly highlights, for individual boys, which areas of work are most important. Within a group setting, common experiences can be dealt with and this in turn highlights individual needs the boys might in fact have.

Another particular issue noted by the group leaders concerned the position of the boys' mothers. It was evident that they had numerous unmet needs and our view is that the effectiveness of groupwork with boys would be aided if work with the mothers took place at the same time.

We would also stress the importance of the role of the boy's key worker. There was some tendency for others involved with the boys to stand back, believing that the group would resolve all the issues. This is clearly not the case and when key workers remained in touch, we found this helped the group process.

It was also noticeable that the boys developed a strategy of using the group to deal with all the personal issues. This resulted in the group leaders focusing, in the final three sessions, on helping the boys to realise that they were strong enough to survive without the group. Our experience was that there was a real need for the group to end on a positive note and that the boys must not go away having their view of themselves as victims reinforced.

Nevertheless the overall conclusion of the experience of running the group was that by having a forum for sharing with others the experience of sexual abuse, the boys were able to begin to tackle many of the major issues that they felt confronted with. The boys reported, and the group leaders felt, that the group did provide a powerful source of assistance and that the whole process of sharing was central to this. Our experience is that the boys themselves recognise that this is a way forward and are ready in fact, to share in a group setting.

This article first appeared in *Practice*, 1988, 2(2)

Three

The forgotten parent:
Groupwork with mothers of sexually abused children

Helen Masson and Marcus Erooga

BACKGROUND AND CONTEXT

During the late 1980s, the Rochdale National Society for the Prevention of Cruelty to Children (NSPCC) Child Protection Team has been developing a package of facilities with the aim of assisting and treating sexually abused children and their families. Groupwork forms a major aspect of the package. As Glaser and Frosh (1988) comment:

> Groups offer particularly suitable settings for helping sexually abused children, their parents and even abusers. This is in large part due to the central defining

characteristic of the group, the collective aspect which offers an alternative experience to the isolation, secretiveness and shame that is central to child sexual abuse (p.130).

This article is about the groups we have run for mothers of sexually abused children. However, as with all the groupwork facilities offered, a range of individual, dyad and family approaches are also available so that the various shared and individual needs of family members can be responded to, by a range of agencies, in sensitive and detailed ways.

THE ROLE OF MOTHERS IN CHILD SEXUAL ABUSE

There has been much debate in the area of child sexual abuse about the role of mothers in terms of their 'contribution' to the abuse. Many writers report that, where children are the victims of sexual abuse, problematic relationships are often observed between these children and their mothers (see, for example, Nelson, 1987; Walker et al., 1988). Specifically it is regularly reported that there is emotional or physical distance and a lack of what are viewed as maternal protective behaviours which 'contributes to the difficulty that children have in breaking out of the abusive bind' (Glaser and Frosh, 1988, p. 44) whether the abuse is intra or extra-familial.

Some family systems theorists have, as a result of the evidence about problematic mother-daughter relationships, developed very detailed models of 'the classic incestuous' family (*e.g.* Furniss, 1984) a feature of which seems to be mother blaming. Such theories have been roundly criticised (see Nelson, 1987) and as Ward (1984) puts it bluntly: 'Even if a daughter does experience her mother as rejecting, neither she nor the mother is asking for the father to rape her'.

In our work with mothers, whilst we are aware that some mothers may have ambivalent relationships with their abused children which need to be addressed, we are clear that it is not non-abusing parents, but the perpetrators of the abuse, who are responsible for what has happened to their children.

THE CRISIS WHICH FOLLOWS DISCLOSURE OF CHILD SEXUAL ABUSE

The type of problems identified above may well be compounded by the state of crisis which occurs in families following identification of sexual abuse. Many mothers will undergo what Murray Parkes (1971) describes as a 'psychosocial transition'. This is defined as:

> ...those major changes in life space which are lasting in their effects, which take place over a relatively short period of time and which affect large areas of the assumptive world.

The disclosure of sexual abuse, and its consequences for a woman who was previously unaware of, or not acknowledging, the sexual abuse of her child clearly falls into this category. Parkes argues that this kind of change forces the individual to give up certain assumptions about the world and their plans for living in it, a process of change usually identified as one of grief and mourning.

The first phase of the process is one of shock and disbelief, characterised by an inability to accept the reality of the loss. In child sexual abuse, this may mean being unable to accept that the abuse has occurred. The second phase may be characterised by starting to accept the reality of what has happened, perhaps accompanied by anger or guilt, possibly about previous parenting behaviour. This is frequently followed by feelings of despair and disorganisation as the reality of the loss comes to be accepted and the implications are understood. In a case of sexual abuse, this may mean the loss of a life partner or gaining an understanding of the damage to a child. The final phase involves a redefinition of self, in which the individual examines her situation and finds ways of developing new coping skills. This stage is painful, as the individual has to relinquish the image of self and relationships which were held prior to the crisis.

Crisis theory (Parad, 1965) indicates that it is often most effective to intervene at a point of crisis. In conjunction with individual work, membership of a group may enable mothers to continue moving through the process of crisis resolution without getting unduly stuck. One of the tasks in our mothers' groups was to help the mothers identify the stage in the process they had reached and to offer the possibility of movement and change.

AIMS OF GROUPWORK WITH MOTHERS OF SEXUALLY ABUSED CHILDREN

It will be apparent that many mothers of sexually abused children suffer from feelings of loss, powerlessness and isolation following disclosure. These feelings may be exacerbated because their relationship with their partner has either ended, significantly changed, or is under threat. Therefore a key aim of the groups was to provide women with an opportunity to share the experience of the sexual abuse of their children with others who had been through a similar crisis. A second aim was to facilitate exploration of the feelings and attitudes associated with these experiences, in relation to themselves, their children and the abusing men. Some mothers of sexually abused children may have a blurred understanding of appropriate sexual boundaries. Therefore the groups tried to provide information on what constitutes sexual abuse and to strengthen awareness of potentially abusive situations, both in relation to their children and themselves. Finally, the groups aimed to provide validation of their experience and feelings, to explore issues of self-esteem and assertiveness, and to allow the women to identify other needs they have and to plan how these might be met.

SELECTION OF MEMBERS
FOR MOTHERS' GROUPS

As Walker, Bonner and Kaufman (1988) point out, there is a great diversity amongst non-abusing parents (usually mothers). They demonstrate that in cases of intrafamilial abuse the likely response of the non-abusing parent cannot be assumed. They described a study undertaken by Myers (1985) of 43 mothers of incest victims, which indicated that:

> ...the mothers fell into three groups: (a) those who denied the incest and took no action (9%); (b) those who rejected their daughters and protected their mates (35%); and (c) those who proceeded to protect their daughters and reject their mates (56%) (Walker et al., 1988, p.157).

Given such diversity, it was necessary for us to develop criteria on which to recruit for the groups. We eventually decided that the group would be open to mothers who were able to acknowledge to an extent (50 per cent at least) that their child(ren) had been sexually abused, whether by a perpetrator inside or outside of the family.

We were aware that mothers who attended our groups had very different personal and family circumstances and that this could have led to difficulties with individual needs being so special or overwhelming that they would find it hard to give and take in a group setting. The selection process involved considering the mothers along this kind of dimension and we always made explicit contracts with them and their key workers (usually local authority social workers) about the basis on which appropriate issues would be referred out of the group back to the key worker. In retrospect, we believe that the diversity of the mothers' situations proved an asset allowing for a range of opinion and experiences which produced lively debates and a variety of views on possible solutions to problems.

When considering selection for a mothers' group, one important issue, which should not be overlooked, is that there are indications (Mrazeck, 1981; Well, 1981 quoted in Kee McFarlane, 1986) that a significant proportion of mothers of children sexually abused within the family have themselves been sexually abused as children. The mother may be unable to deal with her children's abuse until she has had the opportunity to deal with issues about her own abuse. This work was not a primary aim of the mother's groups, but rather was seen as within the remit of adult women 'survivors' groups. Therefore, at the referral stage, if this was identified as an issue then the possibility of joining a survivors' group before becoming a member of a mothers' group was discussed, though we were guided by the women's wishes in this matter.

After an initial selection process, we felt that it was essential to hold a pre-group meeting. Such contact allowed us to further assess the mothers in terms of the recruitment criteria already outlined and gave them a chance to make their own assessment of us. We provided information about the aims, structure and timing of the group and answered their questions as far as we could. Part of the point of such meetings was to reach out and engage with women who often lacked confidence and self-esteem, and whose worlds had recently fallen apart as a result of the discovery of the sexual abuse. Issues of confidentiality and the fact that one of the co-leaders was a male were raised (see below) and, if appropriate, mothers were invited to attend at least the first session of the group in order to evaluate for themselves what they felt they might get from involvement in the experience. This kind of preparatory work is very time-consuming, but we feel that it is essential for getting such a group off the ground.

FEMALE AND MALE CO-LEADERSHIP

The general arguments for and against the involvement of male workers in sexual abuse work have been well rehearsed (Frosh, 1987). We decided to have female and male co-workers and outline here some of the relevant points from our own experience.

During the sessions we found that the women were able to relate to a male worker in a positive way, although there were inhibiting consequences because of the presence of a man. Some of the more uninhibited discussion took place in the absence of the male co-leader, *e.g.* a spirited discussion about what the women would like to do to male perpetrators occurred in his absence. It was also necessary for some women to differentiate the male worker from the men who had sexually abused their children, and indeed from men in general, by the use of such comments as '...but he isn't a man, he's a social worker'.

There were beneficial effects of a male co-worker being present in terms of providing a positive model of maleness. However, an unanticipated advantage was in relation to what seems to be an almost mystical ignorance, or lack of understanding, in both genders about each other's sexuality. Thus, many women accepted the myth of men's uncontrollable sexual urges and need to gain immediate sexual satisfaction. During group discussion about why the men might have sexually abused these women's children, when there was conjecture about men not being able to control their sexual desires or urges, it was powerful to have a man in the group who could assert that those were not sufficient reasons for sexual abuse. Indeed they were only excuses for behaviour about which men clearly had a choice.

TEAM BUILDING AND CONSULTATION

Before starting to run the group, time needs to be set aside to build the worker team (Hodge, 1985; Morrison, 1987; Erooga, 1994). In our own team building efforts, for example, we spent time sharing our respective theoretical frameworks; putting down any baggage from previous experiences of co-working; sharing our liked and disliked leadership styles, our hopes and fears about working with each other; and identifying what we felt were the strengths and weaknesses in our practice skills which we would bring to the work. This does not mean that some unresolved issues will not come up during the life of the group, but the important groundwork will have been done to facilitate the process of dealing with them. In running such a group, we cannot over-emphasise the importance of having outside consultation. The group process will evoke strong reactions in group leaders who may well mirror in their own relationship some of what is happening in the sessions. A consultant who can look at the situation objectively is enormously helpful, if not essential, in analysing what is happening.

STRUCTURE AND PROGRAMME

In setting up the group we drew on various literature sources for ideas about the structure and programme we would adopt. In particular we found articles by Hildebrand and Forbes (1987), Damon and Waterman (1986) and, to a more limited extent, Shearer and Williment (1987) helpful. When planning the first group, and bearing in mind our own time commitments, we decided to offer ten sessions. The group sessions were held in a large meeting room with comfortable chairs for one to two hours every fortnight. We saw it as important that members should feel as welcomed and valued as possible, so we ensured that any pre-briefing or preparations were completed before the first women were likely to arrive. Therefore we were free to welcome them and offer drinks and biscuits as they arrived. Gradually, over the weeks, the women took more responsibility for organising the refreshments, a healthy sign, we felt, that they were taking more 'ownership' of the group. We were willing to assist, in emergencies, with taxi fares or transport in order to facilitate attendance at the group. Such back up services cost money and, in planning for groupwork, the active encouragement of the hosting agency needs to be secured so that resources are available.

As regards the planning of the programme for the group meetings, our reading (outlined above) helped us to identify a core of topics that could usefully be addressed once the important tasks of engagement and contracting (building on the pre-group contacts we had with the women) had been negotiated. These included sessions on:

1. Mothers telling their story about their child(ren)'s abuse.
2. Identifying echoes from the mothers' own childhood experiences and dealing with these.
3. Looking at issues of anger, punishment, fault and responsibility.
4. Exploring mothers' often ambivalent feelings towards their child(ren), about the break up of the family (where this had occurred) and about what had happened to the perpetrators.
5. Offering information about sexual abuse and sex education.
6. Picking up on issues of assertiveness and the right to say 'No'.

We used a variety of treatment techniques to explore these topics, including small and whole group discussions, videos, story-telling and artwork, small experiential exercises and brainstorming. For example, we showed extracts from a video about adult survivors of sexual abuse as a trigger to encourage the women to share their own experiences of abuse both as children and as adults. Short inputs were offered on the theory of psycho-social transitions, on the court process and on the needs of children who have been sexually abused. As issues arose these were brainstormed and analysed and, as well as talking, the women were on occasion encouraged to paint how they were feeling - an opportunity to escape from the trap of repeating familiar phrases. This was greatly enjoyed, after some initial hesitation, and led to reminiscences of school and their own childhoods in a very natural way.

It was interesting that in the second group, the same topics were covered in a very different way than in the first. Perhaps because of our own anxiety and lack of experience in running such a group, for the first group we developed detailed plans for each session (though during the contracting phase in the early sessions we also sought the women's views on what they wanted including before finalising the programme). We then worked hard at keeping to the session plans, sometimes feeling thwarted when mothers brought other 'burning issues' from their current circumstances which took up most of the meeting. It was almost a relief when as a result of discussions with our consultant we gave ourselves permission to relax our enthusiastic leadership efforts, and allow ourselves to be led more by the needs the women brought, as happened during the life of the second group. The mothers in the second group were, in fact, very firm with us that they would say when they wanted formal inputs.

When reflecting on the phases that the groups went through we found the description offered by Hildebrand and Forbes (1987) very useful. They discuss three stages: creating the environment; turbulence and learning; consolidation and learning. However, our experience differed from theirs in that we were surprised by how quickly (immediately) the women wanted to disclose and share what had happened to their child(ren), and we suspect that the pre-group work we undertook before the first session had something to do with this phenomenon.

EVALUATING THE GROUP EXPERIENCE

Early on in the life of the group, we asked mothers to complete self-administered questionnaires on their self-concept (one of a battery of rapid assessment instruments described by Fischer, 1978: see Appendix) and they then completed the same questionnaire during the last session of the group. There was only minimal movement recorded in the women's self-evaluation questionnaires, hardly surprising in view of the relatively short term nature of the groups when viewed in the context of the totality of the women's lives. However, in terms of other criteria - clarity about who was responsible for the abuse of their child(ren); confidence in their ability to parent and protect in the future; and greater certainty about what they would consider as abuse of their child(ren) or themselves - feedback from the women was much more encouraging.

When the mothers were asked for their opinions about the groups they mentioned their regret about the groups ending. It was encouraging that they were able to express their feelings about this so clearly. They particularly valued the support they had gained from each other over the weeks and the opportunity to share very mixed emotions. This was something they said they could rarely do within their own families or with friends.

It was obvious that different mothers used the group for different purposes, some being of a shorter term nature than others, *e.g.* obtaining support through the ordeal of the court process, as opposed to looking to the group for longer term emotional support and social outlet. This would in our view lend support to the idea of trying to resource a permanent group for mothers, with open and closed phases. At one time, during the life of our second group, there was some discussion about some of the mothers attempting to transform themselves into a self-help group. However, this proved to be over-ambitious given the small number of 'hard core' members, their lack of confidence and perhaps too the absence of a tradition of such self-help groups in this country. Nevertheless, we would see this as an important development for the future although, as Glaser and Frosh (1988) point out, their functions will be different from professionally led groups.

CONCLUSION

It is increasingly clear that child sexual abuse has family victims in addition to the abused child. Paying attention to the mothers' needs increases the possibility of them also becoming survivors, and hence the likelihood that their links with their children will be strengthened, within a protective environment. Like so many groupworkers before us, it was humbling for us as professionals to realise that the women had more to offer each other, because of their shared experience, than we could ever hope to, though we are also clear that professional involvement was crucial in providing structure and direction to the group.

APPENDIX

Self-Esteem Questionnaire

Fischer (1978) describes measurement models as 'one of the most interesting innovations in research...to provide regular ongoing feedback to client and worker...' We used one of these designed by Hudson and Proctor (1976) in the form of a self administered questionnaire, the Index of Self-Esteem (see below).

The scale is designed to be answered by the client in a very brief time, to be as simple and non-threatening as possible. It can also be scored by workers in a matter of minutes for simultaneous feedback. Higher scores are associated with, or indicative of, the presence of problems.

The scale is designed to be used as a repeated measure, that is, to be administered at regular intervals 'as a measure for monitoring, assessing and guiding the course of treatment on a continuous basis' (ibid).

Scoring

Reverse score every positively worded item. For example, if the respondent scored such an item as 1, rescore it as 5; 2 is rescored as 4; 4 rescored as 2; 5 rescored as 1; and 3 is left unchanged. After all the positively worded items have been rescored (all negatively worded items are left unchanged) add up all the scores, then subtract 25 from the total.

This method of scoring produces a minimum possible score of 0 (absence of or minimal problems) and a high score of 100 (presence of problems).

Questionnaire

Name: _____ Today's date: _____

This questionnaire is designed to measure how you see yourself. It is not a test, so there are no right or wrong answers. Please answer each item as carefully and accurately as you can by placing a number by each one as follows:

1. Rarely or none of the time
2. A little of the time
3. Sometimes
4. A good part of the time.
5. Most or all of the time.

Please begin:

1. I feel that people would not like me if they really knew me well ☐
2. I feel that others get along much better than I do ☐
3. I feel that I am a beautiful person ☐
4. When I am with other people, I feel they are glad I am with them ☐
5. I feel that people really like to talk to me ☐
6. I feel that I am a very competent person ☐
7. I think I make a good impression on others ☐
8. I feel that I need more self-confidence ☐
9. When I am with strangers, I am very nervous ☐
10. I think that I am a dull person ☐
11. I feel ugly ☐
12. I feel that others have more fun than I do ☐
13. I feel that I bore people ☐
14. I think my friends find me interesting ☐
15. I think I have a good sense of humour ☐
16. I feel very self conscious when I am with strangers ☐
17. I feel that if I could be more like other people, I would have it made ☐

18. I feel that people have a good time when
    they are with me ☐
19. I feel like a wallflower when I go out ☐
20. I feel I get pushed around more than others ☐
21. I think I am a rather nice person ☐
22. I feel that people really like me very much ☐
23. I feel that I am a likeable person ☐
24. I am afraid I will appear foolish to others ☐
25. My friends think very highly of me ☐

Items to reverse score:
3. 4. 5. 6. 7. 14, 15, 18, 21, 22, 23, 25

This article first appeared in *Groupwork*, 1990, 3(2)

Four

Groupwork with sex offenders:

The probation service response

Leah Warwick

This chapter draws on a research project conducted by the author between November 1990 and February 1991. The project was designed to examine the extent and nature of sex offender groupwork conducted by the Probation Service of England and Wales. Beginning with the premise that the establishment of groupwork with sexual perpetrators is in accord with more general practice development within the Probation Service, contemporary groupwork initiatives are described and possible implications for their future development discussed.

WHY GROUPWORK?

A cursory review of professional and practice literature suggests that the response of the probation service to the management of sex offenders has undergone a process of change. There has been a movement from a reluctance to work with sexual perpetrators and the practice of non focused intervention, toward an increasing interest in confronting the problem. This has been facilitated by a wider dissemination of knowledge and the development of proactive practice expertise principally based upon the use of American treatment philosophies. Interestingly, within this trend groupwork has emerged as the preferred method of intervention (Cowburn, 1989; Warwick 1991).

The impetus behind this movement may be seen as three-fold. Firstly, work with sex offenders reflects growing knowledge about the extent and nature of sexual offending and an understanding that imprisonment is an ineffective and potentially damaging response (see for example, Jarvic, 1989; Westwood, 1988). Secondly, increased interest has been encouraged by recent Government directives (in particular the white paper, *Crime, Justice and Protecting the Public*, 1990 and Home Office News Release, 14 February 1991). Whilst these publications stress a continued commitment to the use of custodial sentences for serious sex offenders, they also extend periods of supervision on release and encourage probation services to develop treatment programmes for use in conjunction with probation orders and parole licences. Thirdly, it may be argued that present trends reflect changes in the 'occupational culture' of probation work which has seen movement away from the contention that rehabilitative casework is ineffective (the 'nothing works' perspective), toward a renewed belief that service intervention can exert an important influence on behaviour. This change in professional outlook has gone hand in hand with the development of techniques designed to confront offending behaviour more directly. A growing number of focused treatment packages have now been introduced for use in areas such as alcohol misuse (Baldwin, 1990) and car theft (Hutchins, 1991). In the vast majority of these schemes groupwork has been selected as the core approach (Caddick, 1991). Therefore, the use of groupwork techniques in work with sexual perpetrators can be seen as part of a wider trend in probation practice.

However, the inclusion of sex offending among the behaviours considered amenable to groupwork process does raise important concerns. As is acknowledged by various writers throughout this book, the treatment of sex offenders is an area in which the ramifications (for victim, offender and professional) of inappropriate intervention are known to be profound. Consequently, in minimising the threat to potential victims and maintaining public and government confidence in probation service intervention, a clear conceptualisation of what is both necessary and efficacious in the use of groupwork with sex offenders seems essential.

THE RESEARCH

Reflecting these concerns and in an attempt to widen the existing knowledge base, a research study was conducted during 1990 and 1991 to examine the status of community based groupwork with sex offenders undertaken by the probation services of England and Wales. In this part of the UK the probation service is divided into 55 divisions or individual 'services', each locally run through a management structure headed by a single Chief Probation Officer. Whilst accountable to the Home Office and resourced by a combination of central and local government funding, local decision making exerts considerable impact on the development, direction and application of practice. The potential for diversity this prompts is further enhanced by the fact that wide differences exist in terms of geographical spread, client density and levels of staffing. Anticipating results concomitant with the above and drawing from established findings, the following themes were selected for analysis:

1. How many sex offenders are supervised by individual probation services and what type of supervision do they receive?
2. How many of these services run groupwork programmes for sex offenders? How long have these run and how are they structured?
3. Have these services produced policy statements outlining the style, nature and content of work with sex offenders?
4. Are the services working in collaboration with other agencies and professionals?

The research received backing from the Association of Chief Officers of Probation (ACOP). Data collection was by way of semi structured questionnaire. A response rate of 92% was achieved.

RESULTS

Given the variations in size between different probation services, it was not surprising to find the numbers of sex offenders being supervised ranged from less than 25 in small rural services such as Powys, in Mid Wales to over 400 in large services based in urban conurbations such as West Midlands, West Yorkshire and Greater Manchester.

Table 1
Sex offenders under supervision of the probation service
by type of supervision, 30th September 1990

	n=6247	%
Voluntary throughcare	3048	48.8
Probation	1816	29.1
Parole	480	7.8
Other	903	14.5

Source: Survey of Probation Service in England and Wales

The majority of sex offenders were receiving non statutory supervision from the probation service either in custody or on release from custody (throughcare). A significant proportion were also reporting to the probation service on a statutory basis as a condition of a parole licence or were serving a probation order in the community (see Table 1). Overall, sex offenders constituted approximately 5% of all cases being supervised by the Probation Service.

The number of services who reported specialist groupwork provision for sex offenders was far greater than expected and suggested that the publicised initiatives were more a norm than an exception. 39 (71%) services reported groupwork currently taking place (see Table 2 overleaf).

However, it was interesting to note, that for most services groupwork with sex offenders was a relatively new initiative. Two thirds of those services who said they ran groups, had been doing so for less than 2 years. Only Hampshire, Avon, Nottinghamshire and Derbyshire reported groupwork that had been in operation for more than five years.

For some smaller services such as Powys, Mid

Table 2
Current probation service provision of groupwork for sex
offenders, February 1991

	n=55
Groupwork offered	39
No groupwork offered	12
No response	4

Years groupwork provision in place

	n=55
More than 5 years	4
3-5 years	10
1-3 years	11
Less than a year	11
Don't know	3

Source: Survey of Probation Service in England and Wales

Glamorgan, Warwickshire and Gloucestershire which
cover less densely populated areas, there was clearly
insufficient demand to warrant groupwork. These services
tended either to refer sex offenders to treatment groups
run by probation services in adjacent counties, to refer to
the Gracewell Clinic (an independent, residential service),
or to co-work with clients on an individual basis. Of the
larger services, despite having over 100 sex offenders
under their supervision, only Inner London, South East
London, Merseyside and Cheshire did not currently
provide groupwork for sex offenders. However, in each of
these services, working parties were in the process of at
least reviewing the feasibility of groups.

There appeared to be a broad similarity in treatment
and methods among the areas that undertook specialist

groupwork. 17 services supplied literature to illustrate the content of their work. All of these services adopted an approach based on a multifactor analysis of sex offending (Finkelhor, 1986; Wolf, 1984; 1988: Wyre, 1987). Within a multifactor framework the choice of treatment approaches available to probation services was limited by the skills of officers, the resources that were available and the role and culture of the probation service within the criminal justice system. The most common treatment methods employed by probation services were cognitive restructuring, social skills training and behavioural control techniques. In addition, the influence of feminist theory, which informs much of the victim perspective, and psychotherapy which emphasises the importance of the worker-client relationship was apparent. The main features common to probation service programmes were the use of group dynamics to confront offending behaviour and denial, understand the offence cycle and how to break it, explore power differentials between victim and perpetrator, examine damage done to victims, build internal and external controls to prevent relapse, improve relationship skills and provide sex education. Pure behaviourist methods reliant on controlled laboratory conditions such as aversion and satiation therapy were clearly not feasible, whilst pharmacological approaches tended to be regarded as both unethical and part of the medical not the social work domain. Whole family work tended to be the focus of fieldwork supervision, which was provided by many areas for individual offenders and their families as a supplement to offender groups.

The main differences between services offering groupwork programmes for sex offenders lay in the referral criteria, frequency and intensity of work and the degree to which the groups were run in partnership with other agencies and professionals. Whereas some programmes such as those run in Greater Manchester (Rochdale), Bedfordshire and Cumbria only accepted referrals for child abusers, other programmes such as those run in Oxfordshire, Nottinghamshire and Suffolk accepted men who had offended against women or children. However, the majority of referrals for these latter groups were for men who had abused children. Somerset was the only service to have run a group for indecent exposers and one for men who had sexually assaulted adult women.

All services accepted referrals from a variety of sources, including probation orders with treatment conditions, parole licensees and voluntary attenders. Nottinghamshire was the only service to insist that legal conditions should not be attached to contracts of attendance. One or two services which ran groups in partnership with Social Services or the NSPCC also accepted referrals for men who had committed but not actually been convicted of a sexual offence.

Whereas most services had referral guidelines, these tended to be fairly general. Detailed assessment criteria were less commonly stated. 16 (34%) services reported that assessment of sex offenders was 'always' undertaken by specially trained officers and 21 (46%) claimed that this happened 'sometimes' . In Suffolk all referrals to the sex offenders group underwent a two hour assessment interview which followed a set procedure. Cumbria worked to detailed assessment guidelines which had been jointly written by probation and social services. Other services such as West Glamorgan and Oxfordshire used members of their sex offender advisory groups to undertake assessment interviews, although it was not clear whether standardised assessment criteria were employed.

In most services groupwork operated on a weekly basis, for 2-3 hours. The actual number of group sessions that made up a programme varied quite considerably from 10 in Lincolnshire to over 50 in Cumbria, whilst in Suffolk and Bedfordshire a rolling programme with no limit was offered. As an alternative to weekly sessions, Oxfordshire offered a two week block followed by individual supervision for a minimum of six months and Nottinghamshire offered two one week blocks with a six week gap in between, supplemented by individual casework. West Glamorgan had recently reviewed their practice with sex offenders and were planning to adopt a more intensive programme along similar lines. A prominent feature of most services work was the close involvement of other agencies and professionals. All services reported close liaison with psychological and psychiatric services at least 'sometimes' if not 'always' . Many groups were co-led by probation officers and clinical psychologists (e.g. Norfolk, Durham), psychiatrists (e.g. Kent), social workers (e.g. Lancashire) or NSPCC social workers (e.g. Greater Manchester, Wiltshire).

In East Sussex a multi-agency approach to child sexual abuse was adopted, and perpetrator groups were managed and run by a committee of probation officers, social workers, psychologists and Community Psychiatric Nurses with close links to child care and family services. Northumbria Probation Service were committed to developing a multi-agency approach and had recently created a specialist post to coordinate this task. In Somerset, a multi-agency working party consisting of police, social service departments, psychological, psychiatric services, National Society for the Prevention of Cruelty to Children and probation representatives was in the process of being set-up. Both Berkshire and

Nottinghamshire were seeking to establish a multi-agency strategy for work with sex offenders during 1992.

Few services reported 'always' sharing information about sex offenders with social services and police. In the absence of any clear policy in this area, decisions to share information were often made by officers on a case by case basis. Overall, services' links with social service departments seemed to be more firmly established than with the police. With the exception of Northamptonshire and Cumbria, no service mentioned close liaison with the police.

The majority of services did not have a specific policy statement that outlined the purpose and content of work with sex offenders. Of the seven services who said they did, only North Yorkshire, South Yorkshire and Cornwall's could be regarded as sex offender specific policies. Twenty-one services reported that they were currently in the process of producing a policy statement and practice guidelines for work with sex offenders. This process was just underway in services such as West Yorkshire, Kent and East Sussex where a working group had recently been formed to look into the issue, but in services such as Greater Manchester, Avon, Oxfordshire and Staffordshire the process was nearing completion.

Many services were aware of the need to demonstrate the efficacy of work with sex offenders. However, most were in the process of developing groupwork and were not yet at the stage when issues of impact and outcome were being given primary consideration. The use of self report attitude questionnaires such as the Rape Myth Acceptance Scale (Burt, 1980), Sex Fantasy Questionnaire (Wilson, 1978) and Cognitions Scale (Abel and Becker, 1984), or adaptations of these instruments, were being used in areas such as Oxfordshire, Hereford and Worcester, West Yorkshire and Somerset to measure changes in cognitive distortion; although as a single means of evaluating treatment efficacy these are methodologically problematic. Some areas monitored reconvictions for sex offenders during and after the period of treatment, but the follow up period was invariably less than two years and comparison with a non treatment control group was not made.

DISCUSSION

Though undoubtedly limited in scope this research permits two potentially important conclusions; firstly with regard to current practice and secondly in relation to the implications of such practice upon the future development of probation run perpetrator groupwork. In the first instance it must be said that, in view of the prescriptive uncertainty which still surrounds the treatment of sex offenders, the response of the probation services represents a positive initiative. Furthermore, the service's use of groupwork as a medium for addressing the problem is, of itself, seemingly unproblematic. The utility of the technique is subject to considerable consensus whilst many commentators, including Erooga, Clark and Bentley in chapter 6 of this book outline the advantages to be gained from such an approach. However, what does emerge as significant, however, are questions surrounding, not the objectives to be aimed for, but the form of groupwork most appropriately employed. For though the research demonstrates that groupwork based on multi-factor models is perceived as a viable method, disagreement exists in respect of the structure, duration and intensity of such work. This may reflect an absence of clarity or organisational synthesis within the probation service as a whole. It may also be the case that structural variations reveal understandable anomalies which bear testimony to the complexities inherent in the development of practice certainties within this field. I would go on to suggest that differences may purposefully be seen as potentially complementary components of far broader treatment goals. The growing body of literature on sex offending asserts that the perpetrators of sexual crime are a far from homogenous group. They may be differentiated in terms of offence specialisation, psychological traits or behavioural characteristics (see Marshall et al., 1990 for a useful discussion). Therefore, in improving the efficacy of practice, therefore, a greater understanding of under what conditions, and with which 'types' of offender, specific groupwork formats are best applied, is necessary. Diversity within the probation service is in accord with this objective. However, it is important that diversity should reflect the requirements of specific offender groups rather than the parochial differences of style, commitment or resourcing highlighted by the research. Therefore, exploiting the potential benefits to be derived from the probation service's decentralised and consequently diverse response will require changes in service organisation and practice. The nature of these changes, by whom they should be initiated, and what effects they will bring about, are matters for on going debate. However, certain issues raised by the research suggest potential areas for discussion.

A key outcome of the research centres upon the findings that groupwork initiatives tend to be dependant upon the proactive stance of key individual probation officers, and that many services have yet to reach a stage where policy statements and practice guidelines have been devised and agreed internally. These results imply that there is a need for work to be coordinated better within and between services as well as in partnership with other professionals. There seems also to be a need for improved management direction and commitment. Furthermore, it may be argued that research is required to explore the efficacy of intervention and to determine the utility of different formats. To date little has been done to evaluate the impact that groupwork has had on reducing recidivism. Indeed the comparison of treatment effectiveness vis-a-vis a non, or alternative, treatment control group has not been undertaken in this country despite fourteen years of innovation in some areas.

The probation service may also need to address questions of targeting. For example, should intervention be directed at first time offenders (thereby addressing aberrant behaviour at the earliest opportunity) or focus upon perpetrators at a higher risk of imprisonment (diversion from custody being a principal and long established objective of the probation service)? What also of the special needs of adolescent or female offenders?

Facilitating change may require improved training for those who work with offenders; perhaps in the form of a system of worker accreditation. Indeed, the British Home Office, in a recent thematic inspection clearly stipulates that in order to achieve consistent and high quality intervention, work with sex offenders should be restricted to those probation officers that have received additional specialist training.

Whilst the issues described above are within the probation services ability to influence, others are not. More comprehensive or long term groupwork programmes may require further adjustments to the legal frameworks of probation orders and parole licences which only the government may bring about. Above all change may require an increased level of central funding. Indeed, resourcing may prove to be a critical factor. To date it is unclear whether government support for the use of community based groupwork is drawn from a commitment to reduce sexual crime or a desire to limit public spending. Thus, whilst developments to date are to be applauded, it seems that changes must be considered at practitioner, managerial and governmental levels if consistent, demand led and appropriately resourced, sex offender groupwork is to be achieved.

Five
Work with male sex offenders in groups

Malcolm Cowburn

THEORETICAL BASIS OF THE WORK

The language which we use to describe a problem informs the way in which we seek its solution. Traditionally, the language used in relation to sexual offending has focused almost exclusively on the behaviour of the offender. It has predominantly been the language of law and medicine (particularly psychiatry) and both of these professions have been, and to a large extent remain, dominated by men. Medicine sought to understand sexual offending in terms of illness. A sex offender was a person who had acted 'abnormally', his[1] behaviour was a deviation from the norm and by such behaviour the offender manifested the illness. The victims of the offences were not, in this context, within the parameters of the medical view - save only when the offender had also been a victim himself.

The law also concerns itself solely with the behaviour of

the offender. The law relating to sexual offences and offences against property, have common patriarchal roots (see Ginsberg and Lerner, 1989) which perceive women as the property of men and sexual offences to be violations of men's property. Prior to marriage a female was considered to be the property of her father. At marriage she was 'given away' by her father (or other male relation) to her husband to be - often with additional property, the dowry, to enhance her 'bride price'. Once married the female became a possession of her husband; unable to own property in her own right (until the Married Women's Property Act of 1882 relaxed this aspect of patriarchal control) and unable to refuse the sexual use of her body whenever her husband demanded such - in England, at the present time the law still does not recognise rape within marriage. In defining sexual offences, the victim only appears as an object. For example, in rape the woman was or was not penetrated by the offender's penis and did or did not consent to such penetration. In the process of law, the victim appears only to be denigrated by the process of cross-examination.

The language surrounding sexual offences is largely male concerning itself with male behaviours. The female voice, the voice of the majority of victims of sexual assault is silent. This silencing of the victim is not a new phenomenon. Anna Clark (1987) reveals how this process has occurred and been perpetuated over centuries and has become almost uncritically accepted. However, since the 1960s, the women's movement has been central in asserting the experiences of victims of sexual assault and in challenging the conventional male 'truths' about sexual violence. The central feature of their analysis is that a true understanding of sexual violence can only occur when such behaviour is located centrally with a description of male behaviour (see for example Kelly, 1988).

Research, which has revealed that criminal statistics, with regard to sexual offences only represent a small proportion of offences committed (Finkelhor, 1986; West, 1987), supports this account of sexual offending. For further elaboration see Cowburn (1990).

The work in Nottinghamshire accepts a broadly feminist understanding of sexual offending. The structure and content of the work embodies, in different ways, the following statements:

1. Men are responsible for their sexual behaviour.
2. Male response to sexual arousal is not uncontrollable.
3. Sexual offences constitute a use and abuse of power.
4. Sex offences are rarely isolated incidents and do not 'just happen'.
5. Victims of sexual abuse are harmed by the experience whether or not additional physical violence is part of the offence. Therefore, we would take issue with both practitioners and theoreticians who speak of the 'consensual paedophile' or the 'non-violent sexual offender'. Such terminology minimises the non-physical use of power and potentially ignores the harm and damage experienced by the victim. The use of such language implies an uncritical acceptance of the offender's version of what happened before, during and after the offence, and could collude with both the offender's view of himself and his offending behaviour.

Work with sex offenders in groups in Nottinghamshire has been occurring for approximately eight years (see Eldridge and Gibbs, 1987; Cowburn, 1988). For the purposes of this chapter, I propose to discuss this work in five sections - format, content and structure; style and approach to groupwork; resources - staffing and support; characteristics of the offenders' group; and evaluation.

FORMAT, CONTENT AND STRUCTURE

Since the work began, the format of the various groups has changed considerably. Initially they met once a week for a period of 13 weeks for two hours in an evening. However, it was considered that the impact of the programme on group members was dissipated by short sessions over an extended period of time. Decisions were taken which consolidated and concentrated the programme into longer blocks of time. These decisions were taken with considerable trepidation as the leaders were particularly concerned about the emotional impact on themselves of intensive and extended periods of work. However, whilst accurately assessing the increased pressures upon the course leaders, we failed to take account of the leaders' own resilience and adaptability. In a relatively short space of time, what had been a weekly group for sex offenders was transformed into an intensive ten day (two working weeks), full-time course. Originally the courses occurred only once a year, but as the number of referrals has continually increased they now occur four times a year (twice each in the north and the south of the county). Henceforth in this paper, whilst speaking of the groupwork undertaken, it will also be referred to as 'the course'.

Whilst the format of the groupwork has changed considerably over the years, the basic assumptions about the behaviour of the sex offender, and the aims and objectives in undertaking this work, have remained unaltered.

Briefly, the overall aim in working with sex offenders may be stated as being to reduce the risk of re-offending and to promote in the offender the acceptance of full responsibility for his offence.

In the work with offenders, it is assumed that they will refuse to accept one or more of the following aspects:

1. responsibility for the offence (n.b. an offender may

admit that he committed an offence, but may deny responsibility. Offenders who totally deny that they committed the offence are not accepted on the course);
2. that there was any harm, either short-term or long-term to their victim;
3. that they have any sexuality or sexual feelings (the offence is often described in terms of being an aberrant act of a detached or other wise dormant/deceased organ or impulse);
4. that the offence was not an encounter between mutually consenting peers.

Apart from the above explicit areas of denial it would also be assumed that in the vast majority of cases, the offence was premeditated; that the offender had masturbated and fantasised about the act prior to committing it, and that he had 'groomed' (manipulated) the external environment to ensure that circumstances were favourable for committing an offence (both in terms of the availability of the victim and the reasonable certainty that the offence would not be interrupted). It would also be anticipated that offenders would significantly underestimate the extent and amount of their sexually offending behaviour (research undertaken by Abel and his colleagues in the United States supports this view - see particularly Abel, 1987).

In order to reduce the risk of re-offending, an offender must be able to accept total responsibility for the offence. As implied above, often an offender's initial description of his offence can be characterised as being essentially passive - the incident/offence happened to the offender ('I was seduced'. 'She asked for it...etc.'). One of the objectives in the work is that the clients become able to give an active rather than a passive account of their offence. Other objectives, which are all interlinked, may be briefly summarised. During the work offenders should learn to:

1. recognise the role of sexual fantasy and how to control and modify it;
2. understand their behaviour cycle and how to interrupt it;
3. identify risky situations;
4. become more conscious of the victim's perspective of sexual offences;
5. challenge distorted perceptions of women and children and sex and sexuality;
6. improve their social and self control skills.

However, although the aims and objectives have not changed, the means of attempting to attain them are constantly changing and becoming more focused and sophisticated as knowledge and experience of this group of offenders grows.

When the group was first restructured into consolidated blocks of work, it was intended that in the first week, the focus would primarily be on offence related matters - including the use of victims' accounts of their abuse and its effects on their life - and the second week of the course would focus on lighter material, particularly sex education, and social skills exercises. Increasingly, however, the first and second weeks differ less in content. Much of the social skills material has been replaced with greater concentration on offence related issues especially those concerning masturbation and fantasy and how they relate to an offender's cycle of offending behaviour. Many of the changes in the content of the work have occurred as new workers have become involved in running the courses.

However, the course has never attempted to provide a complete and completed package of work for sex offenders. Leaders have always insisted that workers who refer an offender to the courses have the prime responsibility to ensure that on-going work with their client occurs. A system of three way interviews with the worker, client and a course leader both before, during and after the course have been incorporated into the overall structure of the course to facilitate this process.

STYLE AND APPROACH TO GROUPWORK

At the beginning of every course the leaders make a statement concerning the confidential nature of the work being undertaken. Course members sign an undertaking that they will not discuss any information which they hear during the course with anybody outside (there is the proviso that course members are expected to discuss their own involvement in the course with their probation officers). However, course leaders explain to the course members that there are limitations on keeping information confidential. These limitations are that, if any course member discloses that he is currently committing sexual offences or has in the past committed sexual offences for which he has not been reported to the police, and identifies specific victims of these offences, such information will not be kept confidential. Course leaders indicate that in such circumstances they would report the matter to the police. Hopefully this would be done with the compliance of the offender; course leaders would offer to accompany the man to the police station. However, whatever the man's response such information would be passed on to the appropriate authorities: failure to do so would be to collude with the offending behaviour.

The courses, as the previous section has indicated, have a clear pre-planned programme (see Figure I). There are particular issues which the courses seek to address and each session of the course has clearly defined objectives. The course leaders adopt a style of intervention informed by the assumptions referred to above, which focus on

Figure 1. Outline For Two Week Course

Monday	Tuesday	Wednesday	Thursday	Friday
Week One				
Establishing Trust/ Confidentiality	ABC	ABC	How I Could Have Avoided Offending	Assessment/ Risk
Why We Are Here	Structured Interviews Technique			
Self Assessment Risk Assessment			What Stopped My victim Saying No	Targets/Future Work With Own Worker
Sexual History				
Life Graph			Power Exercise	
Masturbation/ Fantasy Cycle			Picking Up Clues	
Victims Work:		Medical Examination of Victims	Pictures Exercise	
Video/Audio Tapes				
Explain Offence from Victim's Perspective				
Week Two				
Re-Group Re-Cap	4 Pre-Conditions	Distorted Perceptions Pictures Exercises	Ages + Stages Attitudes	Risk Evaluation
Risk		Video Work	Questionnaires+Video Work	3-Ways
Victims	Changing My Thinking	Sex Education	Contraception + Aids	
Work		Sexuality Questionnaires	Attitudes	Targets

offending behaviour and the thoughts and attitudes which relate to this behaviour. The group seeks to address the 'what', 'how', 'where' and 'when' of offending behaviour. It does not examine directly the 'why' of the behaviour. In looking at their offences, it has been found that 'why' questions allow offenders to avoid accepting responsibility for their actions and consequently responsibility for changing their behaviour. Thus the group leaders throughout the course, will be directly challenging and confronting group members' statements in relation to a variety of offence-based issues and their attitudes towards women and children. As already mentioned, the style of the course has also been greatly influenced by social skills training methods and techniques. Although the course has shed much of this material, the basic social skills methods (self-assessment, learning and evaluation) still continue to inform and influence the style of the groupwork.

RESOURCES: STAFFING AND SUPPORT

Changes in the format of the groupwork with sex offenders had major consequences in terms of resources. The number of people leading the groups changed from originally two and then three, to four. Given the sustained intensity of the course, it was considered that four workers (two of each gender) was the minimum number for the work to be accomplished efficiently and effectively. Normally at least two of these officers will have been involved in running a minimum of two previous courses. These workers designed exercises, planned and ran the courses. They also provided a detailed written account of each course, which would be available to subsequent course leaders. Apart from the time actually leading the course, the workers met together three times before the course started. These meetings served many purposes including finalising the course programme; administration (*i.e.* issues to do with finance, equipment, premises and food); team building - workers who have not worked together begin to get to know each other. It has always been considered essential that new workers need to share, both the overall ideology, and accept the aims and objectives of the course. Workers leading the course were/are based in a variety of employment locations within the Probation Service. Until recently they did not receive any help in terms of workload. Workers often rearranged their regular work commitments to enable themselves to lead the courses. Gradually, however, this work is now being recognised as an important and integral part of the task of the Probation Service and attempts are being made to resource it adequately. Teams in which the course leaders are located are given some form of workload relief or additional support whilst the workers concerned are involved in the course.

One item which has remained a constant component of the first week of the course, is that all course members undertake a detailed behavioural analysis of one offence which they accept that they have committed. The analysis is called the ABC. This is an abbreviation for - antecedent, behaviour and consequence - which describes the structural approach taken to the interview. Events, thoughts and feelings prior to the particular offence are examined as are the details of the offence and its consequences to offender and victim. (For an illustration of this technique, see Cowburn et al., 1987). These interviews take at least two hours per course member. The membership of the course is divided into pairs and two workers are allocated to each pair for this session - obviously we have to recruit extra staff for this particular exercise. Usually four other probation officers help throughout these interviews.

In recent years, with an increased number of workers being involved in the work, it was decided that course leaders needed an outside consultant to discuss various issues whilst the work was running. The consultant must have experience of both the courses and more generally the area of sexual abuse. She/he visits the workers one afternoon/evening during the first week of the course to offer help and support. Initially, much of the consultancy time was spent discussing problems related directly to the group members, particularly the various ways in which they avoided responsibility for their offences. Being at one remove from the group members the consultant often helped leaders devise appropriate strategies to overcome these blocks (for example one group steadfastly denied any sexual arousal before, during or after their offences. Another group refused to accept that there were any serious consequences for the victims of their offences). Being able to give a dispassionate oversight on the progress of the course, the consultant has also been able to advise workers about changes in the programme. Recently a consultant has helped workers make the painful decision that they must report one of the group members to the police, because they were aware that he was reoffending.

In recent years, the major issues which have been addressed have related more to the dynamics of leadership. The reason for this change appears to be that as workers are becoming more experienced with many of the practice issues relating to the work they are more confident in resolving issues emanating directly from the work with offenders. When this work started it was undertaken by a small number of people who developed their knowledge and practice together and became familiar with each other's particular style of working. Thus they shared many assumptions and understandings which did not need to be made explicit or explained as they planned and undertook the work (for example, the high level of commitment in time and energy expected whilst the course was running, or the fact that sexist statements and attitudes were challenged, whenever they occurred, throughout the course). However, as the work has developed many new workers have become involved and, at times, communication problems have occurred. The consultant has helped workers express these difficulties and resolve them.

Good communication is particularly important where leaders are relying on their co-workers for support in an area which can be personally demanding. The difficulties are generally simple and related to how communication within the group process should occur. An active role for the male workers in challenging sexist stereotypical statements about women may need to be made explicit. Workers may need to give each other permission to interrupt each other, or they may need help in criticising each other for lack of support, during certain sessions. If these issues are not addressed, an efficient group of leaders cannot develop. If they are addressed workers grow in their ability to trust each other and to express their own vulnerabilities. Thus the leader group develops into a strong, mutually supportive, and effective unit.

Apart from staffing, the most important resource for the course is suitable premises. When the work occurred once a week in the evenings, it could be comfortably accommodated, outside office hours, in one of the larger probation offices in Nottingham. However, by changing the format of the group, premises were required which were both suitable and available during the day. Acquiring such accommodation for a socially unacceptable group of clients posed special problems which can be summarised with the words, stigma, confidentiality, and agency responsibility. There is insufficient space to elaborate on these practical difficulties, except to say that the cost of suitable accommodation is always a substantial part of the overall course budget.

CHARACTERISTICS OF THE OFFENDER GROUP

Courses have occurred with between six and 14 clients; although, the preferred number is eight. The clients' ages range between 17 and 65. All clients are male - owing to the small number of female sex offenders, it has been considered inappropriate to accept referrals of females. There have been a small number of black clients on the course, and although this has not been statistically verified, it would seem that black offenders are under-represented. As the courses are held in the daytime, the majority of the clients are unemployed. However, there have regularly been men attending who have taken leave from their employment to do so.

The courses accept all types of sexual offenders although by far the majority of participants have been offenders against children. Contrary to expectations, pecking orders or hierarchies of offending (i.e. rapists of adult women perceiving themselves to be better than men who offend against children; or men who offend within the family seeing themselves as superior to those who offend outside the family) have never occurred. The issues which we address and the means we use are suitable for all types of offender. Having differing types of offender, in the same group, enables cognitive distortions in relation to specific victims to be more easily challenged.

In the early years of the groupwork, leaders had great difficulty in obtaining sufficient referrals to run a viable group. As the work has changed and become more established, this is no longer a problem. There are regularly twice the number of referrals as there are places available on the courses.

Clients are accepted at any stage of the penal process - pre-sentence, on probation, on parole, on temporary release on licence from prison (*i.e.* serving prisoners) and after release without supervision from prison. The one feature all members have in common is that they have volunteered to attend the course. We strongly resist all statutory conditions to attend the course.

EVALUATION

There are two aspects of evaluation which will be focused upon: firstly the offender's own evaluation of the course and secondly the course as a means of reducing sex offender recidivism.

Offenders' perceptions and comments about the courses have been elicited formally in two ways. In the early years of the work, we asked all course members to complete an evaluation form at the end of the course. The form was designed to address both the relevance of the programme and the way in which it was communicated. The responses contained in these forms enabled workers to shape the course and develop their own presentation skills. Latterly, as the content and structure of the work has become established and workers have become more confident in working in this area, this type of formal evaluation has lapsed. The other means by which we obtain the views of course members is by asking them at the end of each day to mention one aspect of the day's work which they appreciated and one aspect which they resented. Although this is severely limited as a vehicle for obtaining honest and thoughtful feedback, it does have the advantage of being both oral and immediate. One informal indicator of consumer response to the work is the continued level of attendance throughout both weeks of the course - generally this is very high. As mentioned above attendance at the course is voluntary and the vast majority complete the first week and very few fail to return for the second. Group members clearly seem to be committed to attending the course.

Regrettably our approach to assessing the effectiveness of the work as a means of reducing recidivism has been insufficiently rigorous. In the earlier years, one of the group of three leaders assumed responsibility for intermittently checking the probation records of ex-group/course members to ascertain whether they had been reconvicted of a sexual offence. The inadequacy of criminal conviction as an indicator of the presence of offending behaviour has regularly been commented upon. Furby et al. (1989) have revealed in detail, the many methodological flaws of research into effectiveness of 'treatment' and sex offender recidivism. In the light of this review, our casual cursory examination of probation records was probably valueless.

The other type of assessment of the effectiveness of the course has been the systematic use of questionnaires designed to indicate attitudes and attitude change relating to issues surrounding offending behaviour, sexuality and perceptions of women and children.

These questionnaires are filled in by all course members before, during and after work. They may indicate areas of attitudinal change and also highlight areas requiring further work. The original questionnaire was derived from a statement of the aims and objectives of the work. It was designed to reveal changes in expressed attitudes in the following areas : insight into offending behaviour; control over offending behaviour; effects on the victim; child sexuality; relaxation skills. In a recent unpublished study (Wright and Bannister, 1990) of three courses it was found that during the work the vast majority of course members showed significant positive changes in all of the above areas. The least change occurred in the offenders' perceptions of their ability to control their behaviour when sexually aroused. However, as Wright and Bannister point out, at present there is no evidence to support a view that such changes are sustained over an extended period.

In concluding this paper, however, I would wish to highlight the fact that such short-term intensive work with sex offenders in groups highlights more issues than it resolves. Although the area of 'scientific' evaluation is fraught with both practical and theoretical difficulties (see Furby et al., 1989; Quinsey, 1984; 1986), the subjective opinion of course leaders is that during the work offenders begin to accept responsibility for their offences and their consequences. To state this another way, when offenders start the course their perceptions of their offending behaviour could be characterised as being essentially passive - they committed the offence but when they initially speak of it, the victims' behaviour is described in active terms whereas their own actions are almost ignored. By the end of the course most offenders are beginning to own, in an active manner, full responsibility for planning and carrying out the offence and for the harmful consequences of the offence to their victim. Such movement is significant and important but essentially we have thus only begun to engage with the problem. Hopefully in the future, a graded series of courses can be devised to maintain and develop this initial momentum for change.

Note

1. The vast majority of sexual offences are committed by men. I will, therefore, use male pronouns when referring to the sex offender.

This article first appeared in *Groupwork*, 1990, 3(2)

Six

Protection, control and treatment:
Groupwork with child sexual abuse perpetrators

Marcus Erooga, Paul Clark and Mai Bentley

INTRODUCTION

The pressure for good practice is never greater than with child protection issues - the need to translate good ideas into effective intervention. The rational and professional reasons for this are clear: victims are vulnerable and by definition less powerful than their abuser; the possibly physical and certainly psychological/emotional effects of sexual abuse often require lengthy treatment. In working with child sexual abuse (CSA) it has become clear that no one agency can be successful alone - 'good practice' is based on professional co-operation, whilst the consequences of 'poor practice', for children and professionals can be enormous. Several of the issues revealed by the child abuse enquiry in Cleveland can be seen partly as about fracture and breakdown in the multi-agency system.

BACKGROUND AND CONTEXT

Social work has, traditionally, encountered the consequences of social problems in its dealings with clients, but attempts to address the causes have been seen as political action, with heated debate about the relevance or appropriateness of social work addressing them. At a rather different level, how child protection workers are to deal with the perpetrators of the sexual abuse of children has caused a similar conflict. As the prevalence of CSA became clearer during the 1980s so there was a rise in the number of such cases being dealt with by both the child protection agencies - by which we mean those agencies whose primary task is child protection, *i.e.*, usually social services departments (SSDs) and the National Society for the Prevention of Cruelty to Children (NSPCC), and the Criminal Justice agencies: Police, Courts and Probation.

By the mid 1980s, the problem for the child protection agencies had become finding a way off the treadmill of dealing with the consequences of child sexual abuse without dealing with the immediate cause - those men who had already abused children and who would probably do so again if their offending behaviour was not addressed. The research illustrates the extent of the problem. In 1987 a study by Gene Abel, Judith Becker and others was published in America. They interviewed 567 non-imprisoned men known to have committed sexual offences against both adults and children, under the special terms of a legal amnesty. The men could disclose the full extent of their offending without risk of prosecution. They found not only that levels of offending were higher than conviction rates suggested, but that patterns of offending were not as discrete as previously thought. Thus the ratio of arrests to acts for violent crimes was 1:30, whilst that for 'non-contact' offences was 1:150 - indicating the unreliability of using conviction rates to determine incidence. Their research also indicated that the average ratio of offenders:victims was also high - non-incest offenders against girls averaging 1:20 and against boys 1:150 - showing that effective intervention with perpetrators could potentially prevent abuse for a considerable number of children. This is an important consideration at a time when pressure on agency resources make it especially important to target 'efficient' areas of work.

In Rochdale a way forward was for the social work agencies to come together to establish a common understanding of child sexual abuse perpetrators, sharing information and ideas, and determine the most effective form of provision locally. Their decision was to establish a treatment group. The aims of the group would be:

1. to effect change in the men's abusive behaviour to prevent or reduce the likelihood of further offending;
2. to provide information about those men specifically and sexual abuse perpetrators in general to add credence to research;
3. to inform and empower agencies and professionals working with perpetrators.

WHY GROUPWORK?

Since the 'discovery' of child sexual abuse in the 1980s, and especially since the crisis in Cleveland, the treatment of perpetrators in this country has been developing apace. Existing models of working that pre-dated the importation of American theoretical models were generally contained within family dysfunctional perspectives which tended to indicate that, with intra-familial abuse, the family group should be the focus for intervention. The compulsive behaviour theories turned that approach on its head, demanding separate treatment for individual family members before any family-focused work could take place. The perpetrator was then isolated from the victim so that treatment, in whatever form, could be undertaken avoiding further harmful contact before the perpetrator was ready to take responsibility for the abuse. There is now an increasing number of treatment initiatives established across the UK, the majority of which share two basic facets. Great interest has developed in the compulsive behaviour model as a way of understanding sexual abuse and, from our observations, all the new treatment facilities are primarily in the form of groupwork (Barker and Morgan, 1993). Why is this so?

It is our experience that there are many problems with solely using individual work with perpetrators that groupwork overcomes. Despite the best intentions of all professionals, working in isolation increases the likelihood of colluding with the perpetrator. Unlike many other categories of offender, all professionals may have something in common with perpetrators of sexual abuse, by virtue of their own sexual experiences. Uncomfortable though it may be to acknowledge in this context, we are all sexual beings and echoes of our own sexuality are to be found in deviant behaviour that can be disquieting.

Attitudes to the purpose and function of sexual behaviour, attitudes to women (in the case of male workers) and unresolved negative sexual experiences can all impinge on working with perpetrators. Even without these obstacles there can be other difficulties: challenging the perpetrator's denial and levels of resistance, together with aspects of his minimisation, becomes increasingly difficult on a one-to-one basis; it is easier to fall into the trap of thinking that this client is the exception to all the theoretical rules that have been learned, that he is different. Isolated working replicates to some degree the very secrecy within which the abuse was developed and sustained. Ultimately, working individually, in isolation, makes it more likely for the worker to become enmeshed in the perpetrator's view of the world and his abuse.

Groupwork provides the opportunity for co-working, thus diminishing the risks outlined above. In addition, it enables each worker to sound out issues with colleagues and avoid collusion with the distorted thinking that every perpetrator presents. It also enables the group members' uniqueness to be challenged by other group members thereby reducing the workers' helplessness in tackling denial and minimisation.

Working with perpetrators of sexual abuse is demanding and exacts a personal cost for professionals. This can be kept to a minimum by co-working in groups. Team building, planning, de-briefing and team consultations can all be used to real effect. (The impact of work with sexual offenders on the worker is considered further in Erooga, 1994.)

Group dynamics allow for process issues to serve treatment goals of cognitive restructuring, heightening victim awareness, changing attitudes to women, understanding cycles of abuse to develop relapse prevention, decreasing affective isolation and increasing social skills and, to a lesser degree, providing sex education.

What is not being suggested here is that individual work has no place in the scheme of things. Such work, dove-tailed into a treatment programme, has a very real place and can enhance the whole programme if co-ordinated effectively.

MULTI-DISCIPLINARY CONTEXT

The group in Rochdale started as an inter-agency project, with the Probation Service (Criminal Justice) and the NSPCC (Child Protection) as the two lead agencies. However, it was recognised that there were other important agencies that needed to be part of the initiative, and that fundamental to the success of the project would be the local courts.

The magistrates court was seen as being of particular importance, since potential clients were those whose offences were likely to attract non-custodial sentences or where the group was seen as an alternative to short periods of imprisonment (it was recognised that the group was unlikely to be considered a realistic alternative to long prison sentences, although such men are considered for inclusion on parole). With this in mind a joint agency visit was made to the local clerk to the justices, whose co-operation enabled an agreement to be made that all offenders appearing before the magistrates court for offences against children should be subject of a social inquiry report. The effect of this was to ensure that no child abuser was summarily fined or given a conditional discharge and therefore free in the community without at least having had prior contact with a social work agency. It was also hoped that the social inquiry process would be

Figure 1

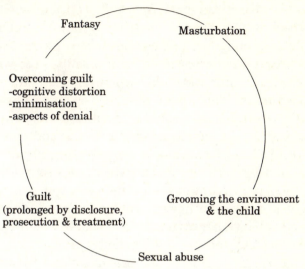

the beginning of an inter-agency assessment and that the two systems, criminal justice and child protection, would thus be linked together.

It was also of central importance that the social services department be involved, as they would have some responsibility toward the children involved. A local 'think tank' brought them into this new network and secured their interest and co-operation. From the beginning social workers have been seen as an integral part of the whole system, and this co-operation took place in an atmosphere of good working practices. Individual social workers had already engaged with probation officers in some joint work and some were training for joint social worker/police investigations.

It is important to stress that there were initial suspicions to break down. Each agency carries myths about the power and influence of other agencies. As with those working with perpetrators, child protection workers are also often affected by their contact with, and responsibility for, the children they work with. Feelings of suspicion, enmity or anger can be picked up from the child and carried into professional relationships - the workers for the perpetrator and child become polarised and mirror the positions of their clients, an unconscious process which can also be an insidious one. It is not uncommon for such a process to initially manifest itself in discussions about the possibility of running a perpetrators group. Child protection workers may feel anxious that resources will be diverted from victims or their families, or not wish to be so closely associated with perpetrators. However, if there is a conscious decision by agencies that this will not happen, if the issues are addressed explicitly and openly, then structures can be agreed for the sharing of information and tasks so that the problems remain with the clients and are not replicated by the workers. Thus, the process of being open and inviting the family social worker to be part of the work with the group can pay dividends in terms of the client not being able to 'play off' one worker against the other. It also recognises that the needs of the victim, as represented by the social worker, come first. Reversing the process, social workers can share the knowledge that sex offenders are not being 'let off the hook' and that other workers are not being collusive or shifting responsibility.

The preparation for the group took a year and with hindsight there were gaps which could have been filled. Possibly most helpful would have been to establish firm agency ownership of the project in a multi-disciplinary management forum, such as the local Area Child Protection Committee (ACPC).

THEORY

Part of the preparation for the group was a review of the different models available to understand sexually abusive behaviour. The one which seemed at the time to fit workers experience best, and which has subsequently been found to be extremely helpful in understanding and treating abusive behaviour, is that based on an compulsion cycle (Wolf, 1983). (See Figure 1.)

Thus, moving from fantasies of sexual contact with children, which has a disinhibiting effect, combined with the reinforcing effect of orgasm, the grooming process makes the situation and the child available for the abuse to take place whilst reducing the possibility of disclosure or discovery. Following the abuse itself comes guilt and possibly genuine disgust and lowering of self-esteem, combined with self-pity and fear of detection - a phase prolonged at the time of discovery and the commencement of treatment. For the abuse to continue it is necessary for the abuser to find ways to overcome the guilt, and this is typically done by using cognitive distortions to justify behaviour and minimise the effects, viewing the victim's lack of overt symptoms as meaning that they are 'OK'. The time taken to go round the cycle is shorter as the abuse becomes more entrenched.

The treatment programme we have developed is based on an understanding of the men's abusive behaviour as compulsive - an awareness they are unlikely to have themselves.

ASSESSMENT AND EVALUATION

One key concept in sexual abuse is secrecy. Without the attainment of secrecy, abuse cannot go on. Perpetrators benefit from secrecy, it allows them to remain powerful and avoid being confronted with their behaviour. If agencies allow that secrecy to be replicated between themselves, then the abuser remains powerful. For example, if the police have information from their interviews that a man has been abusing one child since he was nine, the social worker knows from the child that in fact he and his sister were abused from age six, and the probation officer thinks, from the information available and the charge, that this is an isolated incident, then the abuser is not effectively confronted or dealt with. Without inter-agency agreement at senior management level, it is quite likely that information will remain locked within agencies, either because of 'procedure', suspicion or ignorance. If we are to work together effectively then it is vital that information is shared, particularly that children's accounts of their abuse are known to those working with the perpetrator. However, this information should never be gained by those workers directly from the child. Attendance at case conferences or sight of case conference minutes will provide the information without putting the child through the further trauma of re-interview.

Therefore, at the point of referral as much information as possible is collected. A form will be completed by the referring professional, attaching detailed information about the known offences and also a form completed by the man himself which includes statements about his view of his offences and what work he thinks he needs to do. This information is then studied and some hypothesis about his offending pattern developed.

Prospective group members will then be interviewed by two workers from the group using a semi-structured format we have developed. The man's offending behaviour will be discussed in detail, his understanding of his own behaviour is explored and his ability to reduce the level of denial is assessed and will be an important element of the overall criteria for acceptance. After these interviews (usually two), if accepted, he will be further seen by one worker to take a social and sexual history.

If the man is to be offered a place in the group then the next stage will be a 'contracting' meeting with all the agencies involved with the man and the victim represented. A typical meeting will have the client, his probation officer, a social worker who is working with the child and possibly other members of the family and any other relevant professional, with two workers from the group. A contract is agreed with the offender, covering behaviour in the group, the limits of confidentiality offered, and an opportunity to set the individual man's objectives for work in the group. This meeting also reviews other issues in the contract which extend beyond behaviour in the group *e.g.* contact with the victim, if at all, or more commonly contact with the mother of the victim, often an issue when the abuse took place in the context of a relationship with the child's parent. As failure to comply with those agreements can lead to exclusion from the group, these issues are usually seen by all those involved as relevant to this meeting, as well as serving to emphasise that involvement in the group is closely related to issues outside.

Those who have worked with sexual abuse will be familiar with a feeling of powerlessness which perpetrators can evoke, partly by the power of their denial or distortion, and because of the lack of legal powers to protect children by the removal of the threat (the perpetrator) from the household. Clearly, professionals who experience themselves as powerless in this way may communicate something of this to their clients, either children or parents who already feel powerless by their experience, or to the offender who has already demonstrated his ability to abuse power. For many, the appropriate use of contracting in the group can serve to redress this balance, providing an opportunity for the men to begin to behave in a way which will benefit their previous victims, and for workers to be in control of key areas of treatment.

Throughout their membership, a continual evaluation process of each man is seen as essential to ensure that attendance alone does not become regarded as treatment, to assess progress and attend to issues from within the group which need to be raised in a separate forum or from outside the group which are relevant. Minutes of each meeting are sent to relevant workers, and if there is any indication of renewed risk to a child then child protection procedures can be implemented without delay.

There are also periodic reviews of each man's progress with the original multi-disciplinary group who were convened at the contracting stage. The aim of these meetings is to review progress in relation to the objectives set in the original contract and to set new objectives for the period up to the next review. It will include feedback from staff to other professionals who are working with the man, the victim or the family, about his performance during this period. It ensures that accurate information about work in the group is disseminated and allows them the opportunity to participate in determining new objectives.

At the conclusion of each man's involvement in the group, either because of a decision to leave, exclusion or an agreement that they have benefited as far as they are able to at the present time, this group will be reconvened and a final evaluation undertaken. This will include an opinion about the potential level of risk which he is considered to present and the reasons for this. Other group members are asked to comment, usually summarised as a score out of ten, and it is noticeable that they have thus far been, if anything, more pessimistic than the group leaders about the possibility of reoffending.

It is also made clear at the point of leaving that the final evaluation will be presented to any child protection case conference which may be convened in the future, usually as the result of moving into a household with other children. Thus we are clear, and the man concerned knows, that information about him from the group remains available to the multi-agency forum.

GROUP STRUCTURE

The structure of the initial group was to have direct entry, following the selection process, with the group having closed and open phases. It became increasingly apparent that, following each new intake of men, there was a considerable slowing down of the work of the group, because of the absence of basic group skills in the majority of new members. Therefore we developed a 'feeder' level one group for new entrants to join following the selection process. This level one group is a structured, six session programme covering basic group membership skills and some of the key issues in the main group which the new members will need to address. The structure of each session is the same, two hours with a 10-15 minute break, and is designed to be similar to the structure of the level two group, with similar opening and ending exercises - opening with a round of important news or events since the last meeting and closing with a round of feelings.

Membership of this group also provides the opportunity for further assessment prior to joining the main group and it may be that some men will need to participate in more than one group at this level before 'graduating' to the main group. The programme for the level one groups is as follows:

Session 1. Introductions

Name and offence
Acknowledgement of the effort it has been for many of them to attend today
Ground rules for the group
Statement /description of the abuse they have committed
Closing exercise (round of feelings)

Session 2. Being in a group

Opening round
Ethos of a group - helping others to work; using each other's experiences and perceptions to learn; avoiding collusion
Communication skills - self expression/assertiveness: 'I' statements, being direct, taking responsibility for feelings
Feelings v. thoughts
Closing exercise (round of feelings)

Session 3. Sexual abuse

Opening round
What is sexual abuse?
Normal/abusive behaviour
The cycle of abuse - introduction
Homework - on own cycles
Closing exercise (round of feelings)

Session 4. Feelings

Opening round
What is a feeling? (difference from thoughts)

Identifying feelings - the range of feelings
Expressing feelings safely
Owning your feelings
Closing exercise (round of feelings)

Session 5. Victim awareness

Opening round
Power and control - adult/child
Attitudes
Victim awareness (video of survivors talking)
Homework - relating their cycle to effect on their victims
Closing exercise (round of feelings)

Session 6. Ending

Opening round
Evaluation - self/peers/staff
Preparing for level two/ for another level one and worst fears
Work in the interim period
Closing exercise (round of feelings)

As the level two group runs continuously, the level one group is run on alternate weeks, which involves a considerable time commitment for workers if they are staffing both groups. Therefore a system was developed, whereby the 'core' level two staff team developed the programme and ran the initial level one group. Other workers interested in developing skills in groupwork with perpetrators, but not able to make a commitment to the longer term group, were then invited to run subsequent groups using the structure and programme developed, usually with close involvement of one of the level two staff team to ensure continuity and feedback.

Phase one *(guilt and false motivation)* is usually characterised by an initial presentation of remorse, guilt, embarrassment, self-pity and possibly pre-occupation with the possible consequences of discovery - break up of the family and public shame, exposure to the criminal justice system and possible custody and loss of employment. This often creates a high level of compliance in the group - what might be described as a desire to please, and crucially false motivation. There are often unrealistic expectations about the nature of their problems and the extent of the changes needed; about the time scale of treatment ('I just want to be home for Xmas'); and about the chronic and entrenched nature of their offending behaviour ('All this has been so awful, it will never happen again'). These views, naive though they may appear to professionals, are often sincerely held, and may persist despite attempts to provide a more realistic perspective.

Phase two *(awareness and resistance)* is characterised by a cognitive awareness of the issues and the beginning of an understanding of the work which will be necessary before treatment is complete. In our experience it is often work on victim awareness which has a powerful impact on the men, and moves their thinking forward from a focus on themselves and their own situation to breach the barriers and distortions they have created to block out the effects of the abuse. The effects of this are a shifting of balance in their motivation from having a return home/ reunification as their priority, to seeing the need for treatment in order to avoid relapse, though both elements of motivation will still be present. What is often observed is a parroting of 'correct' responses, in effect more and better compliance, often combined with praise of the therapists. Underlying this, initially, is the absence of real understanding of the issues, or genuine acceptance of personal responsibility, though the desire to be different will be the basis of future work.

Phase three *(awareness and internalisation)* is when beliefs and core constructs change and become owned by the man rather than repeated as correct. Given the long-term nature of the work, early progress towards this phase can be ruled out. This phase represents genuine and sustainable changes of attitude and beliefs and is difficult to evaluate in the short-term. Evidence of real change will need to be sustained over a period of time, and is likely to be a progression, marked by indications of progress and slipping back.

Phase four *(maintenance / relapse prevention)*. We believe that men who have effected real change in their core beliefs will, at this stage, be appropriate for consideration for rehabilitation into a family. At the time of writing none of the men we have seen has yet made sufficient changes to warrant consideration of this, though we are clear that at such time, the interests of the child/ren concerned must be the primary consideration.

It remains to be seen whether a level three group will be viable. Such a group would need to encompass relapse prevention work and an acknowledgement that the risk of relapse is lifelong. The men would be expected to take responsibility for being aware of their own cycle, and to alert professionals if they felt there was a risk of relapse. Rules concerning relationships with children and partners would also be central and specific agreements about conduct would be made.

Throughout the treatment process men may get stuck or not progress beyond early phases. Anger may prevent them from even beginning, or contribute to the stuckness. It is important not to equate apparent motivation, or sincerity about desire to change, with the change itself. It is misinterpretation of this which most commonly gives rise to professional assessments of future risk which describe the offence/s as 'isolated aberrations - not likely to happen again'.

ISSUES

Importance of team building and external consultancy

With any team of group workers, but especially those teams working with perpetrators of sexual abuse, team-building and ongoing external consultancy are essential to develop a staff-group that is able to operate effectively by being aware of each other's strengths and limitations. As with different agencies, different workers can also develop myths about each other which, if not brought to the fore, can inhibit individuals' contributions and functioning.

Each group session can be demanding and stressful, evoking powerful emotions. Therefore the staff group needs to actively create a safe, supportive environment within which to work. Each team needs to seek out skilled consultancy to help in dealing with the co-leadership issues. Such may not be immediately available from within their own line-management structure, and there may be perceived advantages in having this consultation entirely separate from managerial responsibilities.

Gender issues

By the very nature of the work, attitudes to sex, sexuality, children and women will be essential features of groupwork. Group members, all male, will reflect and amplify attitudes that are present in the wider society and these will need special attention within the group. We believe it is essential to have a mixed gender staff team, not least because the mixed gender co-work relationship can be a vehicle for modelling positive male-female relationships. We do not feel it would be acceptable to have only one woman worker in the staff group, because of concerns about her isolation, but female staff members will necessarily be the only females in the room. Therefore, the whole staff team needs to be alert to the differential impact of transactions within the group on their colleagues and each take responsibility for addressing gender issues as they arise. It is important for male workers to avoid being drawn into collusive relationships based on gender and for all to be aware of the possibility of female workers becoming either a focus for the men's anger or being marginalised.

Resource implications

As readers of this publication will be well aware, groupwork is not a way of spreading limited resources more thinly. Groupwork demands considerable planning and debriefing time, and groupwork with perpetrators is especially time-consuming in view of the 'networking' that needs to be undertaken with other agencies, contracting and reviews. The time-scale implications of treatment add an additional resource stress and agency managements need to be aware of this. Management have to view this work as a priority in order to argue for, and allocate, sufficient resources to do the job properly.

Research-led practice

It is important that any initiative in this area has a clear theoretical base and takes account of the available research. We are all subject to 'common sense' notions about perpetrators, and it is by using theory that we can come to 'think the unthinkable' (Wyre, 1990) and so arrive at the reality of the men's offending.

Change of therapeutic style

Anna C. Salter, in her book *Treating Child Sex Offenders and Victims* (1988), refers to the different approach demanded of professionals when working with perpetrators. This is borne out by our experience.

1. *Mandated versus voluntary treatment*: using court-ordered treatment as a spur to motivation has an initial effectiveness on motivation (as will be clear from the discussion above of motivational phases) and can provide statutory controls for the protection of children.
2. *Setting treatment goals*: as social workers we are trained to be non-judgmental and client-centred, and to meet clients' needs. In this area of work it is the professionals who need to determine treatment goals and resist collusion with inappropriate goals which may be unspoken and unacknowledged.
3. *Explicit value stance*: professionals need to set goals based on theoretical assumptions and values.
4. *Setting limits:* the need to take control and limit abusive behaviours is essential. Although this may be uncomfortable initially for some professionals, the need to take control is vital for subsequent protection and treatment.
5. *Limited confidentiality*: professionals need to be clear as to the limits of confidentiality regarding information disclosed in treatment about children abused in the past. These children have treatment needs and the secrecy involved in the abuse is an issue that must be squarely addressed without collusion.
6. *Trust and sex offenders*: we cannot work with sex offenders on the basis of trust. The abuse itself involved a betrayal of trust and, as with other compulsions, to

trust promises, no matter how sincere, is inappropriate. The perpetrator's perceptions will initially be highly distorted. Therefore his accounts cannot be taken for granted as accurate. Verification and information gathering from other sources is necessary.

7. *Respect versus collusion*: finding the balance is important. Meeting the needs of the perpetrator as a person without colluding with distorted cognitions and denial is a challenge for professionals.

8. *Confrontation*: finding ways of challenging without being counter-productive is not always easy. Finding ways to avoid backing the perpetrator into a corner is about finding a style that is essentially enabling as well as confrontative. Control must be exercised with compassion and, as has been pointed out elsewhere, we cannot change these men by punishing them. (Morrison et al., 1989).

CONCLUSIONS

In brief, CSA is a lifelong problem which requires treatment. Groupwork offers a particularly appropriate vehicle for doing this. However, it requires careful planning, resources, a clear theoretical underpinning, teamwork and commitment. The result can be a structure where children are protected and men controlled and treated. (Groupwork with sexual offenders against children is discussed further in Clark and Erooga, 1994.)

This article first appeared in *Groupwork*, 1990, 3(2)

Seven

Group treatment for women sex offenders against children

Sharon Barnett, Francesca Corder and Derek Jehu

There is a very small number of articles on the sexual abuse of children by female offenders dealing with aspects such as its nature and prevalence, the personal characteristics of those involved, and its effects on the victims (Chasnoff et al., 1986; Condy et al., 1987; Faller, 1987; Goodwin and Di Vasto, 1979; McCarty, 1986), but to our knowledge this is the first report of a treatment intervention with women sex offenders against children. This exploratory intervention consisted of a programme of group treatment with six such women who were serving terms of imprisonment for their offences.

Table 1
Demographic and historical data on clients

Client	*Age (yrs)*	*Number of children*	*Known abuse suffered in childhood*	*Known problems in history*
Hilda	23	1	Emotional Sexual Physical	Attempted suicide Psychiatric illness Marital discord
Margaret	43	3		Alcohol abuse Marital discord
Amy	47	5		Non-sexual criminal conviction
Alice	36	4		Alcohol abuse Non-sexual criminal conviction Marital discord
Betty	30	0		Prostitution Marital discord
Sheila	34	2	Emotional	Prostitution Non-sexual criminal conviction Marital discord

CLIENTS

These six clients comprised all the sex offenders against children who were living in a particular part of the prison for their own protection because the nature of their offences was known to other prisoners. Each client signed an informed consent to her participation in the group, and each is referred to by a pseudonym in this article.

All the clients either had never worked outside the home or had been employed in manual occupations. Some demographic and historical data on them is shown in Table 1, but it is emphasised that the information available on any abuse they suffered in childhood and on the problems they have experienced is almost certainly incomplete.

OFFENCES

Two clients were convicted of offences against two children and four clients were convicted of offences against one child. The victims ranged in age from infancy to 15 years when they were abused, and six victims were girls while two were boys.

Two clients were accomplices of male perpetrators, two were co-offenders with both male and female perpetrators, and two were co-offenders with male perpetrators and also independent perpetrators themselves. Thus, all the clients were co-defendants.

The client was the natural mother of six of the victims, in one case she was the victim's sister, and in another she was a friend of the victim's family.

The male and female perpetrators with whom the clients were involved either as accomplices or co-offenders were related to the victims as follows:

1. natural fathers   4
2. stepfathers   2
3. natural mother   1
4. client's cohabitee   1
5. brother-in-law   1
6. friends of family   6

The range of sexual activities in which the clients engaged with the victims included:

1. manual and oral stimulation of the victim's genitals by the clients;
2. manual and oral stimulation of the client's genitals by the victim;
3. penile-vaginal intercourse;
4. insertion of objects into vagina and anus;
5. sexual activities between children while parents watched;
6. participation in pornographic videotapes and photographs.

A similar range of activities occurred between other perpetrators and the victims, the only addition being penile penetration of the victim's anus by the perpetrator.

The prison sentences in respect of the sexual offences ranged from two to four years for the clients, and from three years and six months to ten years for the other perpetrators.

INTERVENTION

The group was led by two women therapists (SB and FC) and it met for ten sessions each lasting approximately one and a half hours.

Session One

The following objectives for the group were elicited from the clients 'to look at our offending behaviour; to change the behaviour; to protect children; and to look at our feelings, attitudes, and beliefs'. The therapists added 'to reduce the risk of reoffending'.

Certain ground rules for the group were established concerning confidentiality, openness and honesty, mutual trust, group identity, commitment to the group, and no discussion outside the group.

Each client was given a private book in which to express her ideas and feelings between sessions and, if she wished, these could be shared with other members of the group at the next meeting.

At the end of this and subsequent sessions, each client filled in an evaluation sheet describing her reactions to the meeting. The comments on this first, introductory session were very positive and no serious negative reactions were reported. This was consistent with the observation by the therapists that no undue distress was apparent.

Session Two

To facilitate later discussion of their sexual offending the clients were encouraged to name body parts and sexual acts using both street terms and more conventional language. The clients were then asked to look at ways in which they minimised, justified, and denied their offending. Many of them said they were under the influence of alcohol or subject to coercion from another perpetrator, and there was a strong tendency to block off and forget what happened.

Next, the clients were led to accept responsibility for their offending, to acknowledge that they had misused their power over children, and to express remorse for having done wrong. This viewpoint was acted out in roleplays in which the clients performed the parts of perpetrator and child. All those present experienced intense distress during this exercise.

Despite these reactions the clients' evaluations of the meeting were generally positive, some found it enjoyable, and several indicated acknowledgement of the need to confront their abusive behaviour however upsetting this might be for them.

Sessions Three and Four

The clients recognised a number of predisposing factors that had contributed to the build up towards their sexual offending, including anxiety and fear, boredom and depression, aggravation and irritation, interpersonal conflict, loss of control, and lack of concern often accompanying alcohol consumption.

Against the background of these predisposing factors there were certain precipitants for the sexual offending including suggestions, persuasion, threats, and force from others; and disinhibition associated with the consumption of alcohol.

Situational factors which facilitated the triggering of the abuse included a relaxed social atmosphere commonly involving drinking, or conditions which had been deliberately planned by a perpetrator to enable the abuse to take place. These situations most usually occurred in the clients' own homes and often involved partial or complete undressing, sometimes after a child or adult had been bathing or showering.

Next, the clients were led to discuss several alternative strategies they might have pursued in these situations to avoid committing their offences. These possible alternatives included:

1. refusing to allow the abuse or to participate in it;
2. leaving the situation themselves;
3. removing the child and seeking protection and support from someone else.

The clients then roleplayed these alternatives. They found this exercise and the whole discussion of alternative strategies to be somewhat difficult and painful, perhaps because it highlighted their perceived powerlessness, inadequacy, and failure to pursue such alternatives in the actual abuse situation. Consequently, the content of the third session was continued in the fourth, with special emphasis on the skills of being assertive rather than aggressive or passive in difficult situations.

The comments on the evaluation sheets for both sessions again were generally positive, but were also much more extensive and revealing than those for previous sessions. The following are some illustrative extracts from these comments:

> *Sheila*: I liked the new found feeling of freedom of not being alone with the pain and guilt...I feel that the group is helping us to help each other and come to terms with the past...The events of the night of the offence are very much in my mind as a jigsaw puzzle of snatches remembered, those that came up during police questioning, and those revealed in court. But I have found through the group that although I cannot piece together as a whole what happened...I can remember how I felt and the general atmosphere, and how the others appeared to be feeling...I feel I could and should have stopped what took place and that as a mother of the victim it was my place to do so...

> *Amy*: I was very upset in today's meeting and also I was so very ashamed and disgusted with myself because I know such terrible things happened to my children. I really hate myself because this could ruin both the life of my son and daughter...In the group I want more of what things to avoid so that this sort of thing will never happen again to any of us but also what to do if we see

other people doing this...Several months ago I made a great mistake and now I'm scared to death...I don't know what to do for the best...it is so very sad to think of so many other children suffering in the same way as my two did so I hope that many people can get the same help as we are.

Session Five

Each client was asked to prepare a family tree and a developmental history of significant events in their lives. Many reported fond memories of grandparents who had been important people in the family. Only two of the six clients had experienced unhappy events as they grew up, in each case with their mothers. In particular, only one client acknowledged having been a victim of child sexual abuse herself. Thus, such victimisation was clearly not a necessary or even a prevalent pre-condition for becoming a sexual abuser in this client group, a finding that was contrary to the therapists' expectations. However, it is interesting that all the women had extensive experience with males who sexually abused children. Each client had her first sexual encounter with an abuser, and each had married or cohabited with an abuser. Three clients had married or cohabited with two different abusers.

The group then performed a roleplay in which one client acted as a police officer who tried to get to know a family secret from the other clients, all of whom played various members of a family. The secret was that the father was abusing the children.

The comments on the evaluation sheets appeared to indicate some confusion about the purpose and content of this session, perhaps because shortage of time prevented completion of the tasks which were to be continued as homework.

Session Six

The group brainstormed the effects of sexual abuse on victims. In the short term these effects were identified as physical damage; fear of adults (men in particular); guilt; lack of trust; emotional upset and damage; nightmares; and confusion about their own sexuality (especially boys). In the longer term the effects were seen to be:

1. inability to form good relationships;
2. fear;
3. suicidal tendencies;
4. anger because they were not believed, were betrayed, or not protected;
5. loss of identity and confused role boundaries;
6. grieving over loss of a normal childhood.

Next, the clients watched a videotape on child sexual abuse including the personal accounts of victims in which they referred to the inability of their mothers to protect them. This experience was quite distressing for all the clients, many of whom were quite shocked to realise the impact of abuse on children.

This was reflected in the evaluation sheets which included comments such as:

> *Hilda*: I found the video very disturbing and the discussion after and before quite upsetting and hard to take in. I blame myself too and I'm angry towards my mother for letting my stepfather use me.

> *Amy*: I now understand what terrible things we all put our children through and how much pain and suffering they have gone through.

> *Alice*: Today's meeting upset me. To see and listen to the children being interviewed was very disturbing.

Just to think it could have been my daughters being interviewed in the same way.

Sheila: I liked watching the video and through it discovering once again just how much my standards and judgement have changed for the better...I disliked the enormous proportion of offences the video revealed...I can now imagine myself even more easily in the victim's place and feel for the victim and the horrors they must suffer...I did not enjoy today's meeting because it made me think of the lasting damage I could be responsible for, and sad for each and every victim of abuse and the lasting troubles they can have years afterwards...I am frightened to think I could have caused serious emotional problems that could last for life in my daughter...I now think differently to the way I used to, I realise things I thought of no harm then, do have an effect on the attitudes of youngsters, and if I was now faced with many of the situations that have taken place my reactions would now be different.

Sessions Seven and Eight

At this point the clients reviewed their experience of the group to date and said that:

1. it had been informative, supportive and helpful;
2. they were feeling more relaxed in talking about their offences;
3. they were more confident, expressive, and assertive;
4. their understanding of abuse was enhanced;
5. the group had helped to make sure that they did not offend again;
6. they accepted responsibility for their behaviour.

During the remainder of session seven and in session eight the clients engaged in several assertiveness training exercises. These were designed to help them distinguish between aggressive, assertive, and passive behaviour; to give them permission to be assertive; and for them to experience how it feels to behave in this way.

On the evaluation sheets most of the clients indicated that they had benefited from the assertiveness exercises, although it had been difficult for several clients. In some cases the revelation of this inadequacy was a source of distress.

Session Nine

This started with two clients disclosing for the first time their involvement in the sexual abuse of children which had not been the subject of criminal proceedings.

The remainder of this final session was devoted to the requirements of parole; the implications of being a Schedule One offender; the roles of social workers and probation officers; the reinforcement of alternatives to abusive behaviour; and the use of supports in the community, which was illustrated by one client from her experiences on pre-parole home leave.

On the evaluation sheets the clients expressed appreciation for the information and orientation they received in this session, and several added positive comments on the group experience as a whole.

Session Ten

The major purpose of this session was a mutual evaluation of the group treatment by the therapists and the clients. The therapists provided feedback to the clients on their progress, and the clients discussed the value of the group to them (see 'Outcome' below).

Table 2
Number of clients endorsing items on Cognitions Scale
(Abel et al., 198) as 'agree' or 'agree strongly' (N=6)

Item		Pre-Treatment n.	Post-Treatment n.
19	My daughter (son) or other young child knows that I will still love her (him) even if she (he) refuses to be sexual with me	5	1
6	Sex between a 13-year-old (or younger) child and an adult causes the child no emotional problems	3	0
10	Most children 13 (or younger) would enjoy having sex with an adult and it wouldn't harm the child in future	3	0
23	My relationship with my daughter (son) or other child is strengthened by the fact that we have sex together	3	0
5	If a 13-year-old (or younger) child flirts with an adult, it means he (she) wants to have sex with the adult	3	0
12	Sometime in the future, our society will realise that sex between a child and an adult is all right	3	0
3	A child 13 or younger can make her (his) own decision as to whether she (he) wants to have sex with an adult or not	2	0
14	An adult just feeling a child's body all over without touching her (his) genitals, is not really being sexual with a child	2	0
15	I show my love and affection to a child by having sex with her (him)	2	0
21	If an adult has sex with a young child, it prevents the child from having sexual hangups	2	0
25	The only way I could do harm to a child when having sex with her (him) would be to use physical force to get her (him) to have sex with me	2	0
18	A child will never have sex with an adult unless the child really wants to	2	0
7	Having sex with a child is a good way for an adult to teach the child about sex	1	0

24	If a child has sex with an adult, the child will look back at the experience and see it as a positive experience	1	0
1	If a young child stares at my genitals it means the child likes what she (he) sees and is enjoying watching my genitals	1	0
4	A child who doesn't physically resist a adult's sexual advances really wants to have sex with the adult	1	0
8	If I tell my young child (stepchild or close relative) what to do sexually and they do it, that means they will always do it because they really want to	1	0
11	Children don't tell others about having sex with a parent (or other adult) because they really like it and want to continue	1	0
16	It's better to have sex with your child (or someone else's child) than to have an affair	1	0
17	An adult fondling a young child or having the child fondle the adult will not cause the child any harm	1	0
20	When a young child asks an adult about sex, it means that she (he) wants to see the adult's sex organs or have sex with the adult	1	0
26	When children watch an adult masturbate, it helps the child learn about sex	1	0

Table 3
Total scores on Cognitions Scale (Abel et al., 1984)

Client	Pre-Treatment	Post-Treatment
Alice	65	113
Sheila	84	119
Amy	84	112
Margaret	100	106
Hilda	106	122
Betty	119	125

The opportunity was also taken to boost the clients' self-esteem and to reward their efforts by praise, encouragement, and a cream cake tea (a rare treat for a prisoner), as well as to exchange goodbyes with them.

OUTCOME

The therapists' records of the sessions and the clients' evaluation sheets as exemplified above contain several indications of therapeutic improvement including:

1. enhanced understanding of the predisposing, precipitating, and situational factors that contributed to the clients' sexual offending;
2. acceptance of responsibility for what they had done;
3. negative emotional reactions to abusive behaviour by themselves or others;
4. greater understanding of the adverse effects of child sexual abuse;
5. development of assertive rather than aggressive or passive ways of coping with difficult situations.

Before and after attending the group the clients completed the Cognitions Scale (Abel et al., 1984). This instrument measures distorted beliefs held by sex offenders to justify their abuse of children (see Table 2 overleaf). Agreement with an item on the scale indicates that the client holds such a belief. Table 2 shows that treatment was followed by a reduction in the number of clients who agreed with each item. At termination only one client still agreed with only one item (number 19).

Lower table scores on the Cognitions Scale indicate distorted beliefs, while higher scores reflect more accurate thinking. Table 3 shows that treatment was followed by higher scores for all six clients, and this improvement was statistically significant at the 5 per cent level (N=6, T=0, one-tailed hypothesis; Wilcoxon test).

DISCUSSION

To the extent that the outcome described above is based on the evaluation sheets and cognition scales it is important to recognise that such self-reports are subject to biases on the part of the clients. They may have distorted these reports in order to present themselves in the best possible light, and sex offenders are reputed to be particularly prone to such dissimulation. Some estimate of the validity of self-reports can be made by examining their consistency or discrepancy across different sources of information. In the present study there does appear to be reasonable consistency across the evaluation sheets, cognition scales, and therapists' records on each client. Moreover, one has to acknowledge that self reports are the only possible means of obtaining information about a client's thought processes, including her beliefs about child sexual abuse.

The crucial measure of outcome is whether the clients commit further sexual offences against children. At present there is no way of predicting such long term recidivism from the data available at the termination of short term interventions. Thus follow-up studies are essential, and they need to be long term because it has been shown with male sex offenders that the longer the follow-up periods, the greater the proportion of offenders who will have committed another crime (although not necessarily a sexual offence). Moreover, as it is estimated that no more than 10 per cent of sex offences are reported to the police, the longer the follow-up the greater the chance of re-offending being discovered. For the same reason, it is desirable to seek measures of recidivism that are more accurate than official records (Furby et al., 1989). Such long term follow-up studies require considerable resources and they are well beyond the aims and scope of the exploratory intervention described in this article. Even if such long term outcomes are ascertained it will be difficult to distinguish the contribution to them of specific treatment programmes and of many other factors such as arrest, court appearance, imprisonment, and various life events.

Despite these caveats concerning the outcome of the group programme, it seems to have been a worthwhile intervention on at least three grounds. First, the clients found it helpful to them in the ways described in session seven. Next it appears to have been accompanied by changes in their understanding, beliefs and attitudes, which prima facie reduce the likelihood of them sexually abusing children in the future. Finally, it constitutes an initial, innovative step in the development and evaluation of effective treatment programmes for women sex offenders against children.

Acknowledgements
The authors wish to thank all the clients whose willing participation and cooperation made the group possible and to acknowledge the support of our prison, probation, and social work colleagues, especially John Bullivant, Celia Cotgreave, Sandra Heald, Jim Loban, Elizabeth Porter, Bobby Print, Beryl Smith and George Walker.

This article first appeared in *Groupwork*, 1990, 3(2)

References

Abel, G., Becker, J., Cunningham-Rathner, J., Rouleau, J., Kaplan, M. and Reich, J. (1984) *The Treatment of Child Molesters*. Available from SBC-TM, 722 West 168th Street, Box 17, New York, New York 10032.

Abel, G.G., Becker, J.V., Mittelman, M., Cunningham-Rathner, J., Rouleau, J.l. and Murphy, W.D. (1987) 'Self reported sex crimes of non-incarcerated paraphiliacs', *Journal of Interpersonal Violence*, 2(1), pp.3-25.

Baldwin, S. (1990) *Alcohol Education and Offenders*. London: Batsford.

Barker, M. and Morgan, R. (1993) *Sex Offenders: A Framework for the Evaluation of Community-Based Treatment*. Available from Home Office Library, 50 Queen Anne's Gate, London W1H 9AT.

Blanchard, G. (1986) 'Sexual molestation of boys idenification and treatment', *Protecting Children*, Fall.

Burt (1980) 'Cultural mths and supports for rape', *Journal of Personality and Social Psychology*, 38(2), pp.217-14.

Caddick, B. (1991) 'Using groups in working with offenders', Groupwork, 4(3), pp.197-214.

Chasnoff, I.J., Burns, W.J., Schnoll, S.H., Burns, K., Chisum, G. and Kyle-Spore, L. (1986) 'Maternal-neonatal incest', *American Journal of Orthopsychiatry*, 56, pp.577-580.

Clark, A. (1987) *Women's Silence, Men's Violence: Sexual Assault in England 1770-1845*. Pandora.

Clark, P. and Erooga, M. (1994) 'Groupwork with men who sexually abuse children' in Morrison, T., Erooga, M. and Beckett, R.C. (eds.) *Sexual Offending Against Children: Assessment and Treatment of Male Abusers*. London: Routledge.

Condy, S.R., Templer, D.I., Brown, R. and Veaco, L. (1987) 'Parameters of sexual contact of boys with women', *Archives of Sexual Behavior*, 16, pp.379-393.

Cowburn, M. (1988) 'Working with male sex offenders', *NAPO (National Association of Probation Officers) Newsletter*, December 1988 - January 1989.

Cowburn, M. (1989) 'Working with sex offenders', *NAPO News*, 6.

Cowburn, M. (1990) 'Assumptions about sex offenders', *Probation Journal*, 37(1).

Cowburn, M., Eldridge, H. and Gibbs, P. (1987) *Nothing Much Happened: Structured Interviewing with Sex Offenders*. Videotape available from Nottinghamshire Probation Service.

Damon, L. and Waterman, J. (1986) 'Parallel group treatment of children and their mothers' in McFarlane, K. et al. (eds.) *Sexual Abuse of Young Children*.

Eldridge, H. and Gibbs, P. (1987) 'Strategies for preventing reoffending: a course for sex offenders', *Probation Journal*, 34(1).

Ernst, S. and Goodison, L. (1981) *In Our Own Hands*. The Women's Press Ltd.

Erooga, M. (1994) 'Where the professional meets the personal' in Morrison, T., Erooga, M. and Beckett, R.C. (eds.) *Sexual Offending Against Children: Assessment and Treatment of Male Abusers*. London: Routledge.

Faller, K.C. (1987) 'Women who sexually abuse children', *Violence and Victims*, 2, pp.263-276.

Finkelhor, D. (1986) *Child Sexual Abuse: Sourcebook*. Sage.

Finkelhor, D. (1987) *A Source Book on Child Sexual Abuse.* Sage.

Freeman-Longo, R.E. (1986) 'The impact of sexual victimisation on males', *Child Abuse and Neglect,* 10.

Frosh, S. (1987) 'Issues for men working with sexually abused children', *British Journal of Psychotherapy,* 3(4).

Furby, L., Weinrott, M.R. and Blackshaw, L. (1989) 'Sex offender recidivism: a review', *Psychological Bulletin,* 105(1), pp.3-30.

Furniss, T. (1984) 'Conflict-avoiding and conflict-regulating patterns in incest and sexual abuse', *Acta Paedopsychiat,* 50, pp.299-313.

Giarretto, H. (1989) 'Community based treatment of the incest family', *Psychiatric Clinics of North America,* 12 (2).

Ginsberg, E. and Lerner, S. 91989) *Sexual Violence Against Women: A Guide to the Criminal Law.* Rights of Women.

Glaser, D. and Frosh, S. (1988) *Child Sexual Abuse.* London: Macmillan/BASW.

Goodwin, J. and Di Vasto, P. (1979) 'Mother-daughter incest', *Child Abuse and Neglect,* 3, pp.953-957.

Hildebrand, J. and Forbes, C. (1987) 'Groupwork with mothers whose children have been sexually abused', *British Journal of Social Work,* 17(2), pp.285-303.

Hindman, J. (1989) *It's All Relative. Family Incest Treatment.* Unpublished Paper Presented at the Fourth Annual Treatment Conference in South Carolina, 21 February 1989.

Hodge, J. (1985) *Planning for Co-leadership. A Practice Guide For Group Workers.* Groupvine.

Home Office (1991) 'John Pattern announces new provision for the supervision of sex offenders', *HMSO News Release,* February.

Hudson, W.W. and Proctor, E.K. (1976) 'A short-form scale for measuring self-esteem' cited in Fischer, J. (1978) *Effective Casework Practice.* McGraw Hill.

References

Hutching, C. (1991) 'The Telford Motoring Offenders Education Project', Groupwork, 4(3), pp.240-248.

Jarvis, M. (1989) 'Who gains from segregating sex offenders?', *Community Care*, September.

Kelly, L. (1988) *Surviving Sexual Violence*. Polity Press.

Maltz, W. and Holman, B. (1987) Sexuality concerns of male incest survivors, *Incest and Sexuality*.

Marshall, W., Laws, D. and Barbaree, H. (eds.) (1990) *Handbook of Sexual Assault: Issues, Theories and Treatment of the Offender*. New York: Plennum Press.

McCarty, L.M. (1986) 'Mother-child incest: characteristics of the offender', *Child Welfare*, LXV, pp.447-458.

Morrison, T. et al. (1987) *Surviving in Teams Is Not Always Easy: A Survival Manual for Teams*. Rochdale Child Abuse Training Sub-Committee.

Morrison, T., Bentley, M., Clark, P. and Shearer, E. (1989) *Treating the Untreatable: Groupwork with Intra-Familial Sex Offenders*. London: NSPCC Occasional Paper.

Myers, M.H. (1985) 'A new look at mothers of incest victims', *Journal of Social Work and Sexuality*, 3 (213) pp. 47-58.

Nelson, S. (1987) *Incest: Fact and Myth*. Edinburgh: Stramullion Co-operative Ltd.

Parad, H.J. (ed.) (1965) *Crisis Intervention: Selected Readings*. Family Service Association of America.

Parkes, C.M. (1971) 'Psychosocial transitions: A field for study', *Social Science and Medicine*, 5, p.103.

Pierce, R. and Pierce, H.C. (1985) 'The sexually abused child: A comparison of male and female victims', *Child Abuse and Neglect*, 9.

Quinsey, V.L. (1984) 'Sexual aggression; studies of offenders against women' in Weisstub, D. (ed.) *Law and Mental Health: International Perspectives*. Volume 1. New York: Pergamon.

Quinsey, V.L. (1986) 'Men who have sex with children' in Weisstub, D. (ed.) *Law and Mental Health: International Perspectives*. Volume 2. New York: Pergamon.

Reinhard, M.A. (1987) 'Sexually abused boys', *Child Abuse and Neglect*, 11.

Rogers, C. (1984) 'Clinical intervention with boy victims of sexual abuse' in Stuart, I.R. and Green, J.G. (Eds.) Victims of Sexual Aggressions, Men, Women and Children. New York.

Salter, A.C. (1988) *Treating Child Sex Offenders and Victims: A Practical Guide*. Beverly Hills, California: Sage.

Sebold, J. (1987) 'Indicators of child sexual abuse in males', *Social Casework*, Feb.

Sgroi, S. (1982) 'Treatment of the sexually abused child' in *Handbook of Clinical Intervention in Child Sexual Abuse*.

Shearer, P. and Williment, S. (1987) 'Taking a risk: group work with families at risk', *Practice*, 1, pp.15-26.

Walker, C.E., Bonner, B.L. and Kaufman, K.L. (1988) *The Physically and Sexually Abused Child*. Pergamon.

Ward, E. (1984) *Father-Daughter Rape*. The Women's Press.

Warwick, L. (1991) *Probation Practice with Sex Offenders*. Probation Monographs, University of East Anglia.

West, D.J. (1987) *Sexual Crimes and Confrontations: A Study of Victims and Offenders*. Gower.

Westwood, S. (1989) 'Sex offenders need help too', *Social Work Today*, December.

Wolf, S.C. (1984) *A Multifactor Model of Deviant Sexuality*. Mimeograph, North West Treatment Associates, 315 West Gale Street, Seattle, Washington 98119.

Wilson, G. (1978) *The Secrets of Sexual Fantasy*. London: J.M. Dent.

Wright, P. and Bannister, J. (1990) *Interpretation of Nottinghamshire Probation Service Courses for Sex Offenders Evaluation Sheets*. Unpublished CQSW Project, Sheffield Polytechnic.

Wyre, R. (1990) *Working With Sex Offenders*. Conference Report, 29 March 1990, Suzy Lamplugh Trust, London.

Notes on Contributors

These notes reflect the status of the contribtors at the time they wrote the articles included in this book.

Editor

Andrew Kerslake, together with Allan Brown, was the co-founder of the British and European journal *Groupwork*. He is currently Director of the Social Services Research and Development Unit at Bath University. The Unit engages in teaching, research, consultancy and the development of software information systems for social workers. SSRADU produces the CHIAC system, a computer based child protection information system which is in use throughout England, Wales and Northern Ireland.

Other Contributors

Sharon Barnett, Probation Officer, Cheshire Probation Service, HMP and YCC, Styal.

Mai Bentley, Senior Probation Officer Working, Court Welfare Office, Rochdale. She was one of the originators of the Perpetrators Treatment Group and has worked with sex offenders since 1986.

Paul Clark, Probation Officer, Rochdale. He has been involved in working with child sexual abuse perpetrators since 1986 and has undertaken training in this area. He is co-author of a book about the assessment and treatment of perpetrators.

Francesca Corder, a social worker, Wirral Social Services Department.

Malcolm Cowburn, a Probation Officer, has been engaged in focused work with sex offenders for many years. He has undertaken research on work with sex offenders in prison.

Eileen Craig, a social worker and Child Protection Officer , Rochdale NSPCC. She has co-led groups for child sexual abuse victims of all ages and has worked in the area of assessment and treatment of families where child sexual abuse has occurred. She also has extensive experience of training in these areas.

Marcus Erooga, Deputy Team Leader, Rochdale NSPCC Child Protection Team, where he has been involved in the Child Sexual Abuse Treatment Programme, initially co-running groups for mothers of victims and, later, groups for men who have sexually abused children. He is an experienced trainer and co-author of a book about assessment and treatment of perpetrators.

Steve Handforth, a social worker employed by the NSPCC and many years experience in the field of child abuse, including being a team member of the Manchester Special Unit.

Derek Jehu , Professor of Clinical Psychology, University of Leicester and Consultant Clinical Psychologist, Leicester General Hospital.

Alex Leith, a social worker with the NSPCC, who has many years experience of child abuse work, including being a Team Leader, NSPCC Stockport Child Protection Team.

Helen Masson, Senior Lecturer at Huddersfield Polytechnic and course leader of the CQSW course. During 1987-88 she completed a ten month full-time secondment as a team member of the Rochdale NSPCC Child Protection Team, during which time she co-led two groups for mothers of sexually abused children. She is co-author of a publication on investigating physical abuse and neglect.

Leah Warwick, Probation Officer in Newbury. The research she describes was conducted as part of her MSc thesis at Oxford University.